A photojournal of a Trini on a Journey

Wide Angles from a Tiny Window

Paula Obé

All rights reserved. No part of this publication should be reproduced without consent of the author/Photographer

Copyright 2020 Paula Obé

All photographs copyrighted by Paula Obé

ISBN: 9798611483749

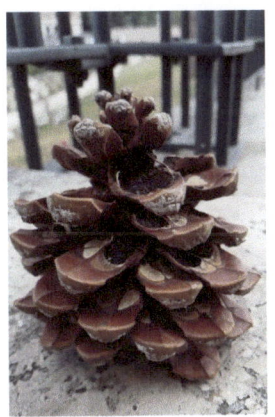

Every journey begins with a single step

I would like to thank my best friend for awarding me this opportunity to be her travel buddy,
and encouraging me to take that leap forward. Thank you Carol Hosein.
Much thanks must also go to Francois for being our guide through much of France.
Also to my co-worker Michelle, for redirecting my misguided commas.

There are some journeys that either change, teach, nurture, seduce, hurt or age you. Some do a little bit of each. This year together with my bestie, I visited Europe for the first time, mainly France and Italy. The scenes in these photos captured pieces of me, so although it was an outward journey, it largely became an inward one.

I have documented some of these thoughts and sentiments in my blog, that carries the same name of this photojournal. They can be divided in several groups, Religion, Cities, Mountains, Monuments & Sceneries. This is my journey... I invite you to share it with me.

Paula Obe

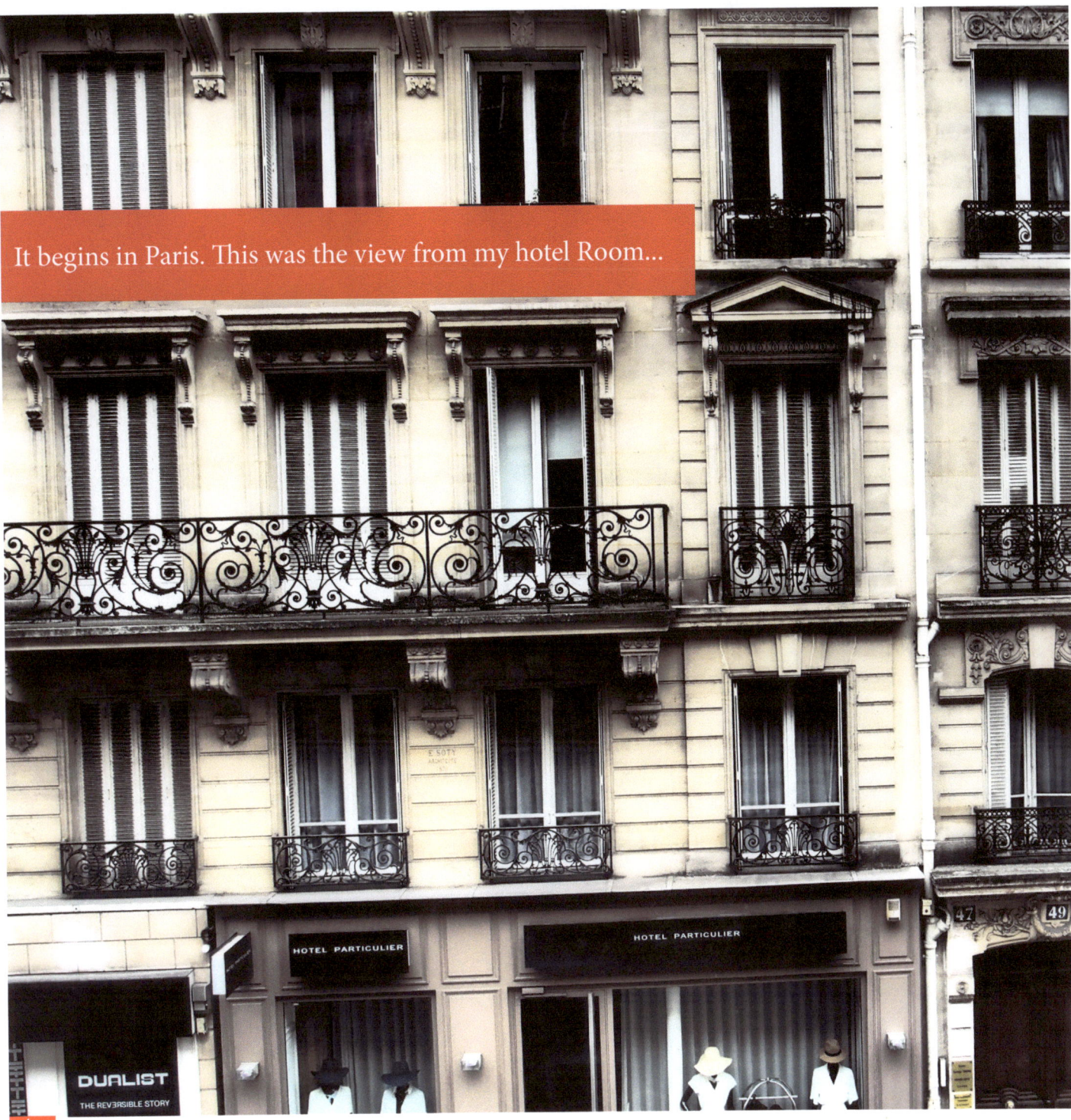

It begins in Paris. This was the view from my hotel Room…

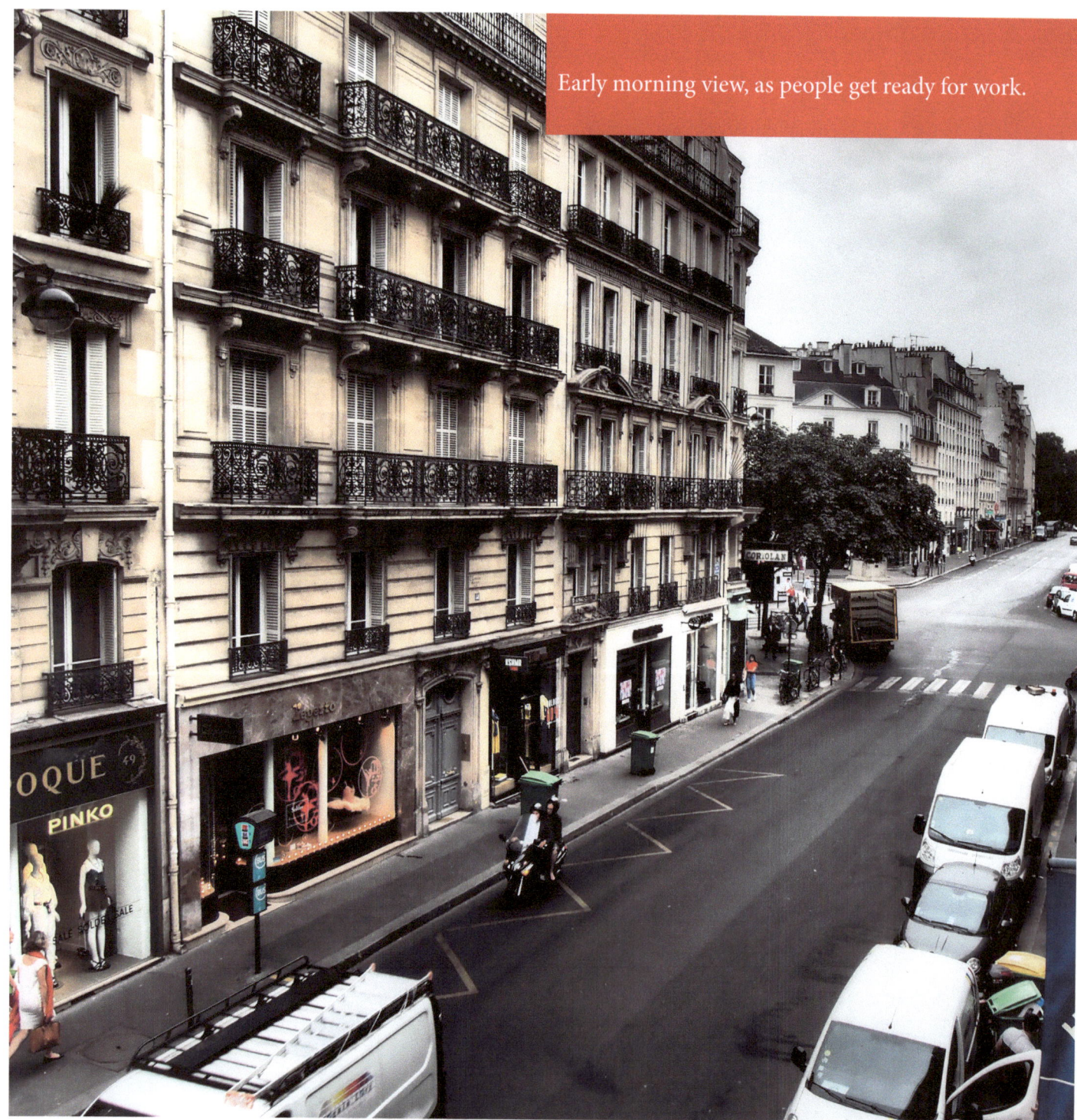

Early morning view, as people get ready for work.

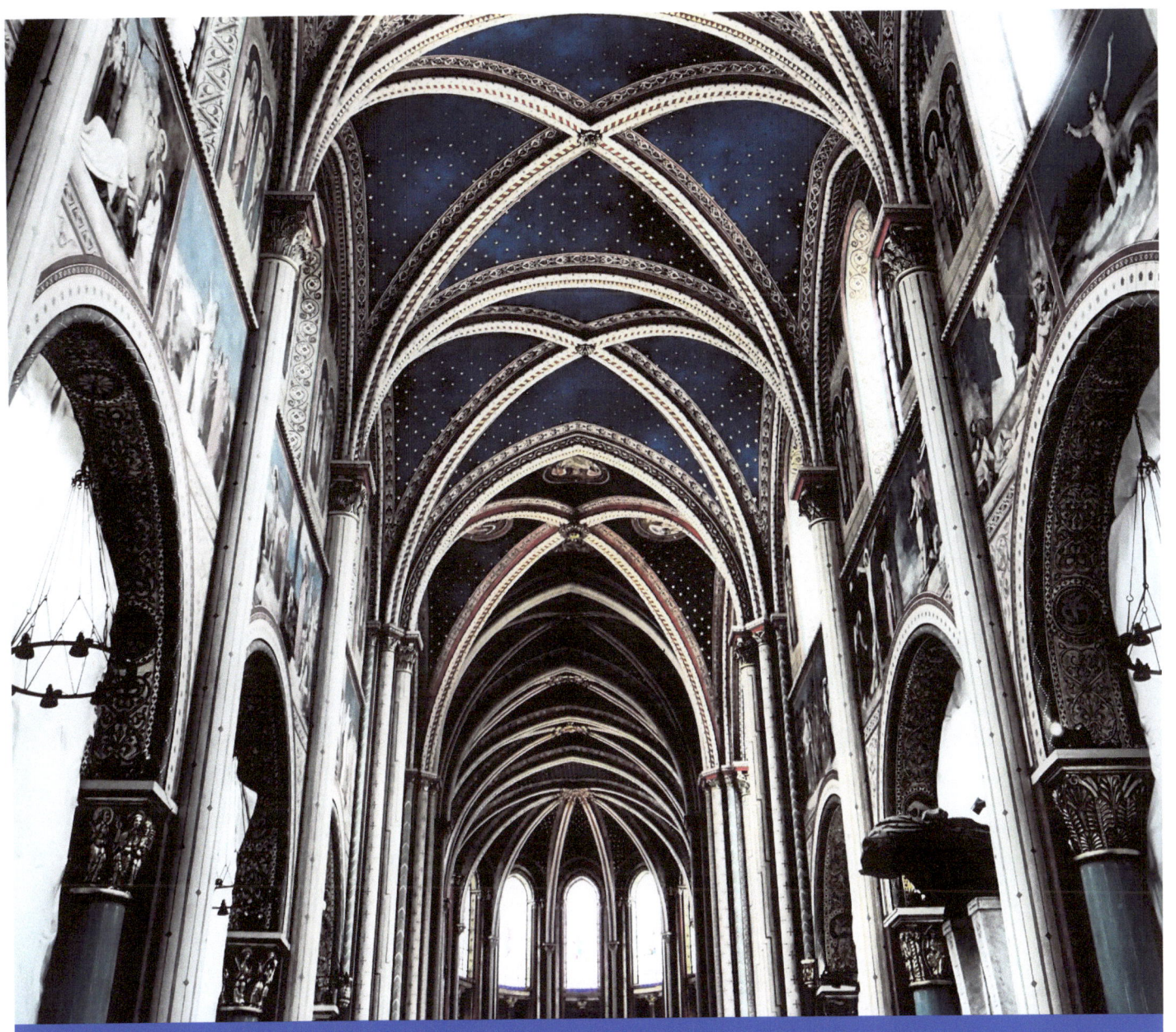

The Benedictine Abbey of Saint-Germain-des-Prés was founded in the 6th century, it is the oldest church in Paris.

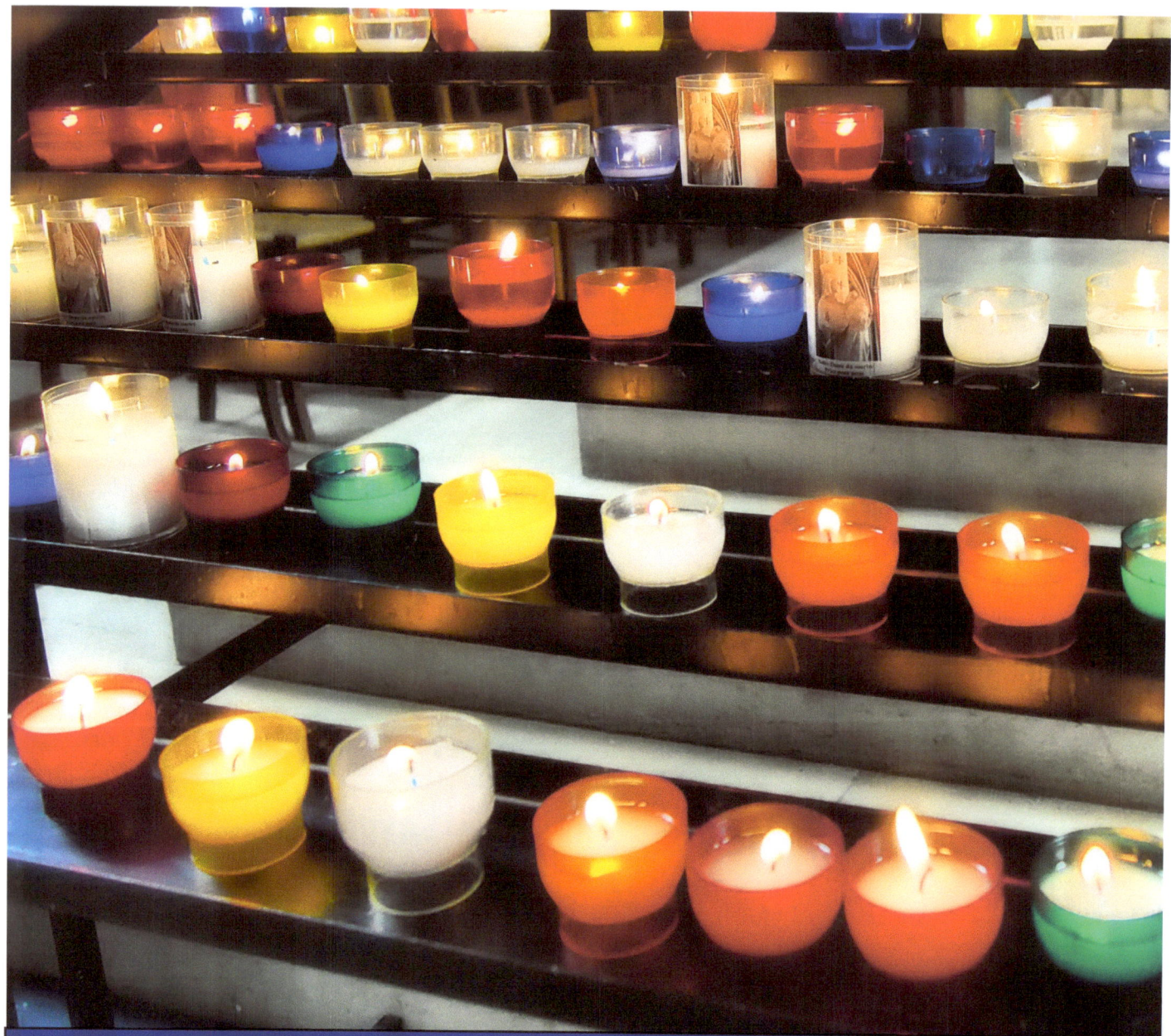

There were two women from Greece, a man from London and a family from India lighting candles, praying in their own way.

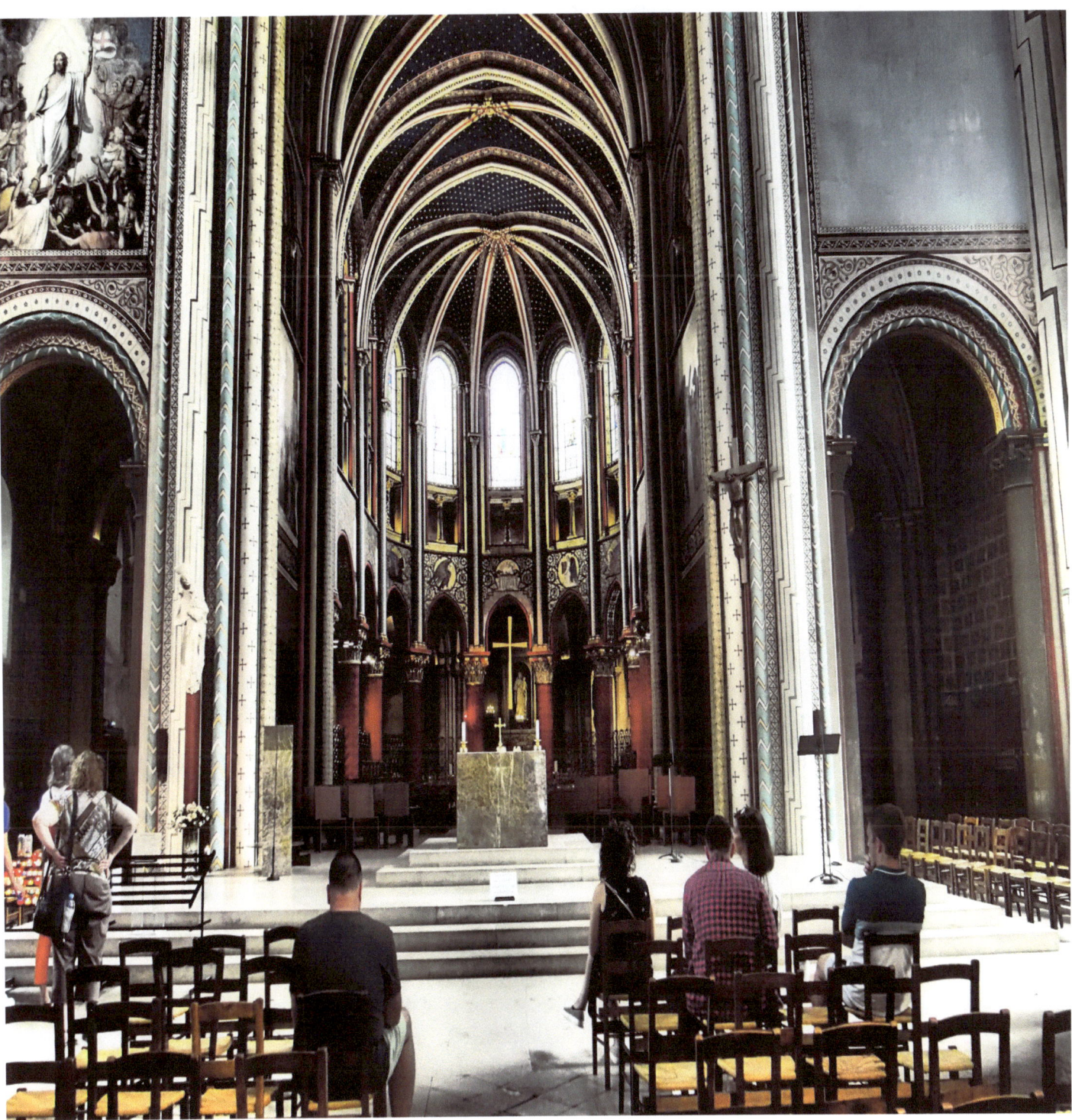

We continued walking from the Abbey of Saint-Germain-des-Prés, enjoying the sights along the way.

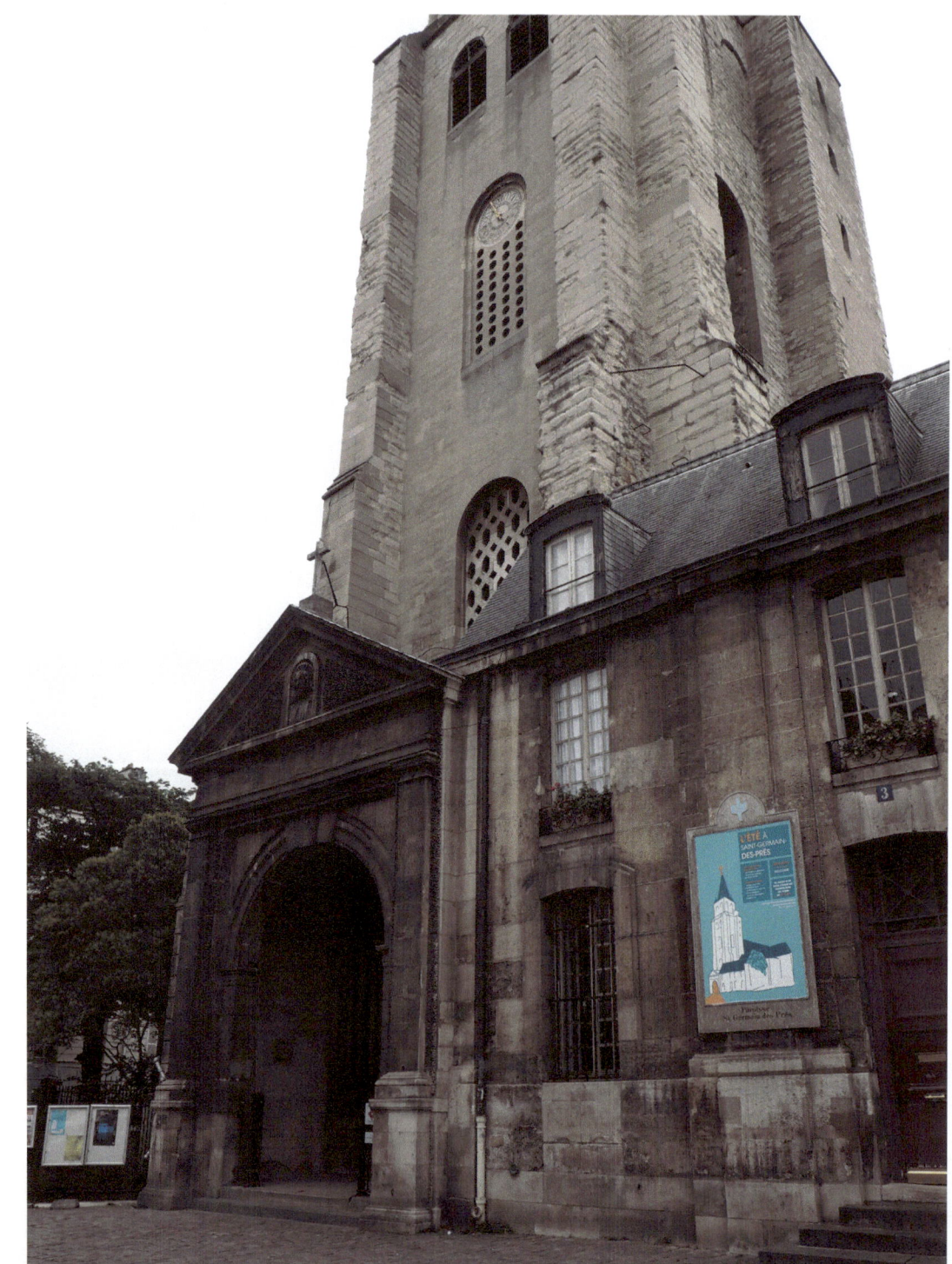

When the darkest hour is in the middle of the day... the clowns come out to play.

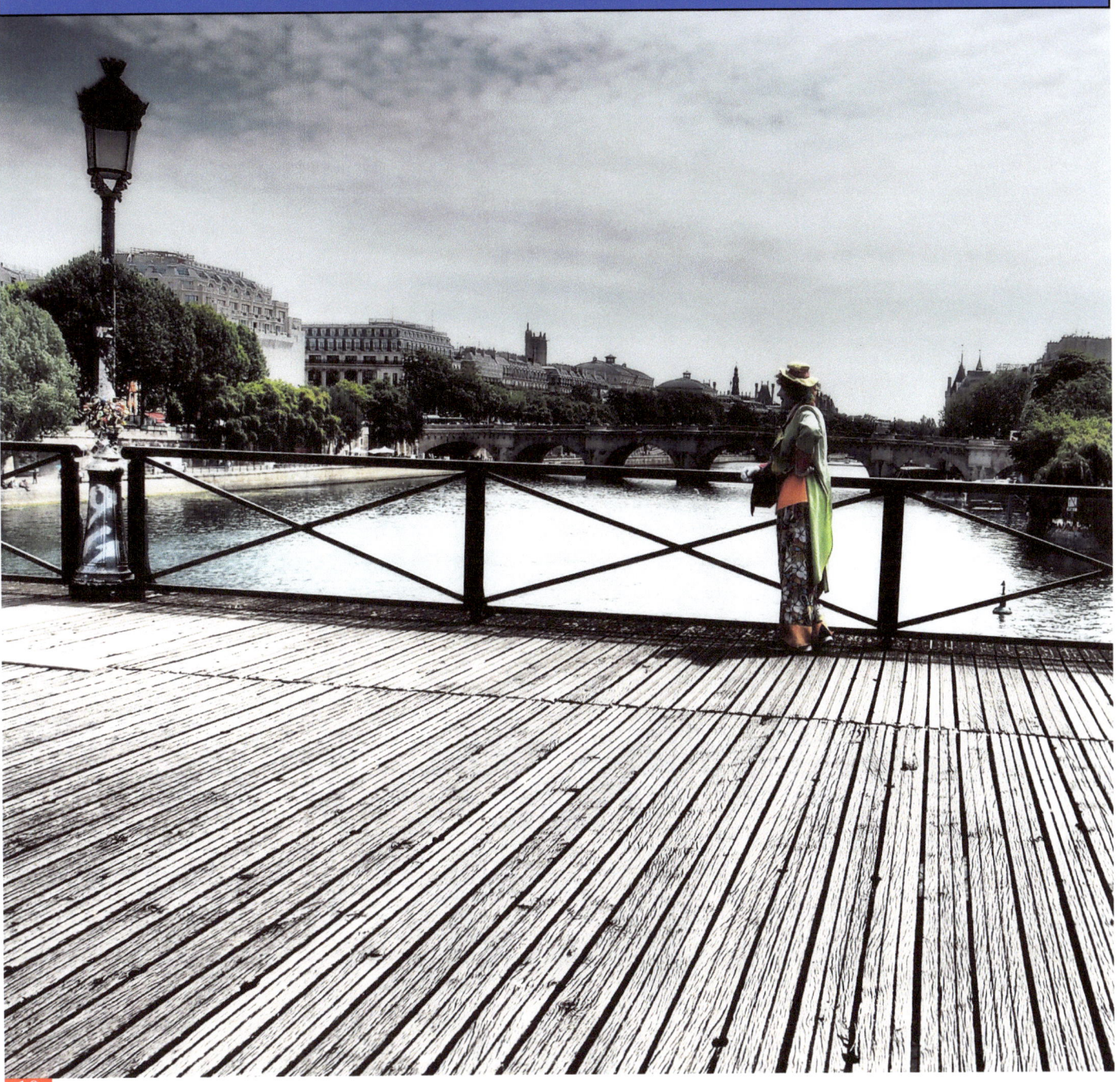

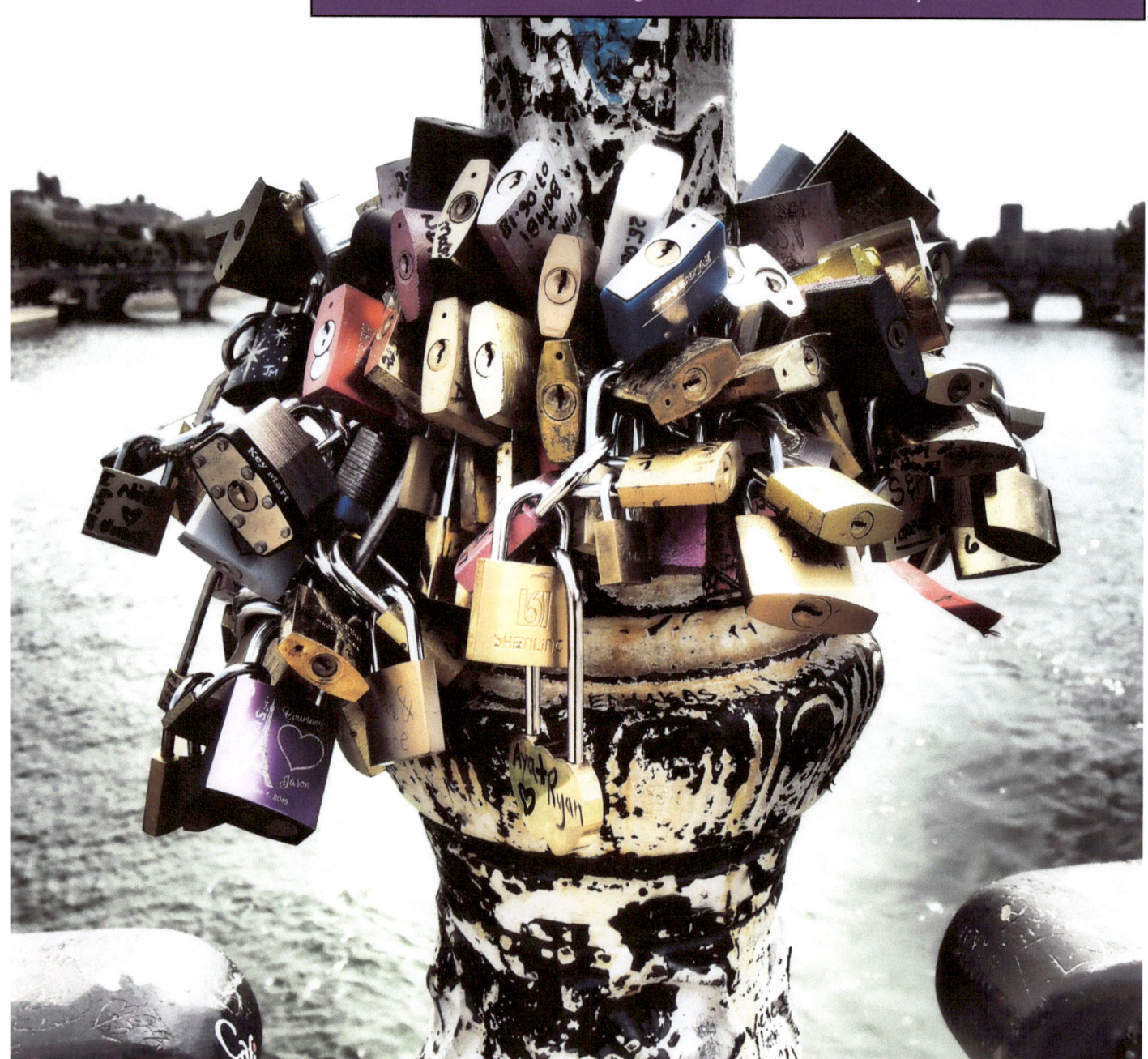

These locks were every where on light poles around the River Seine. Some see them as a disgrace, others see them as a symbol of love.

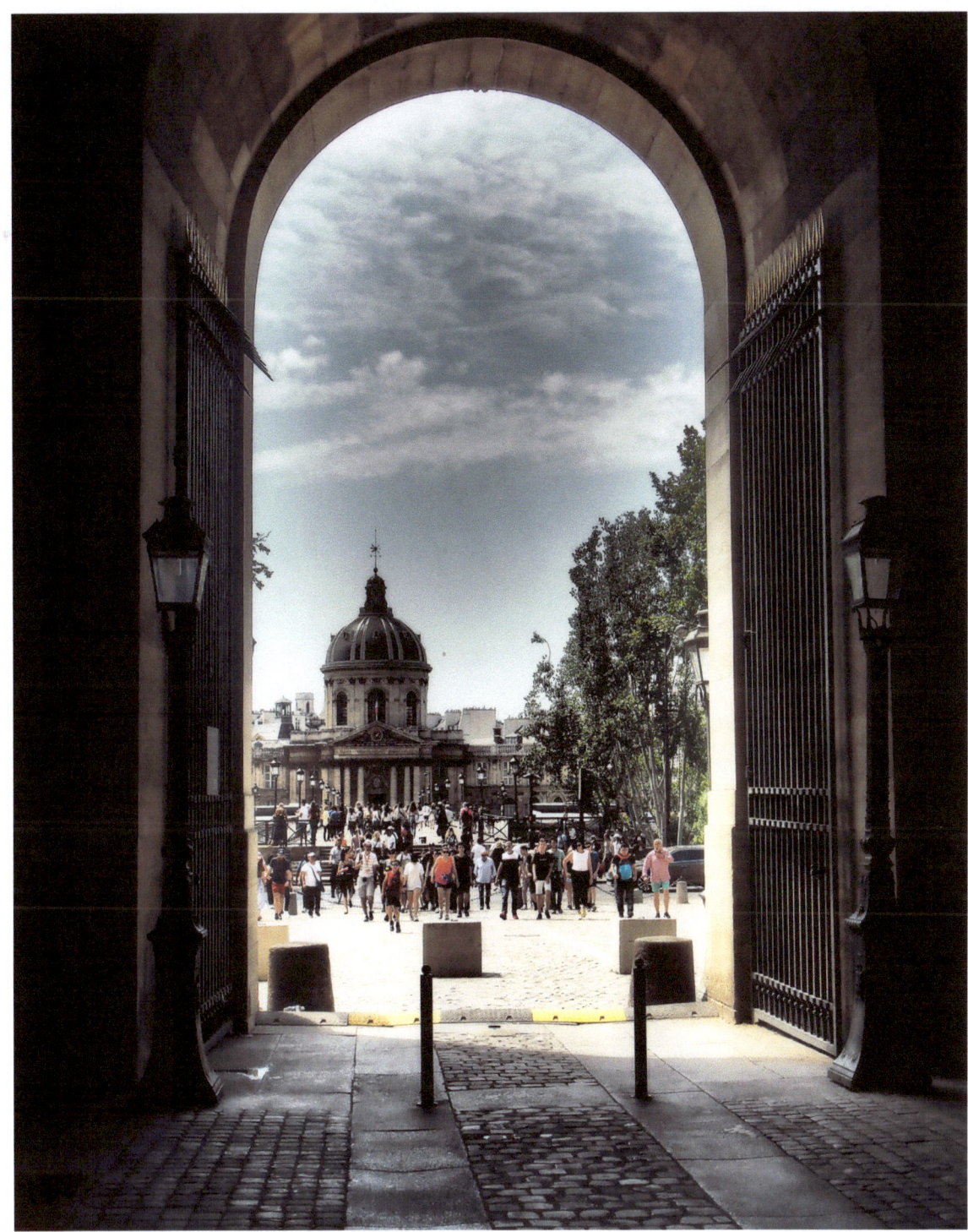

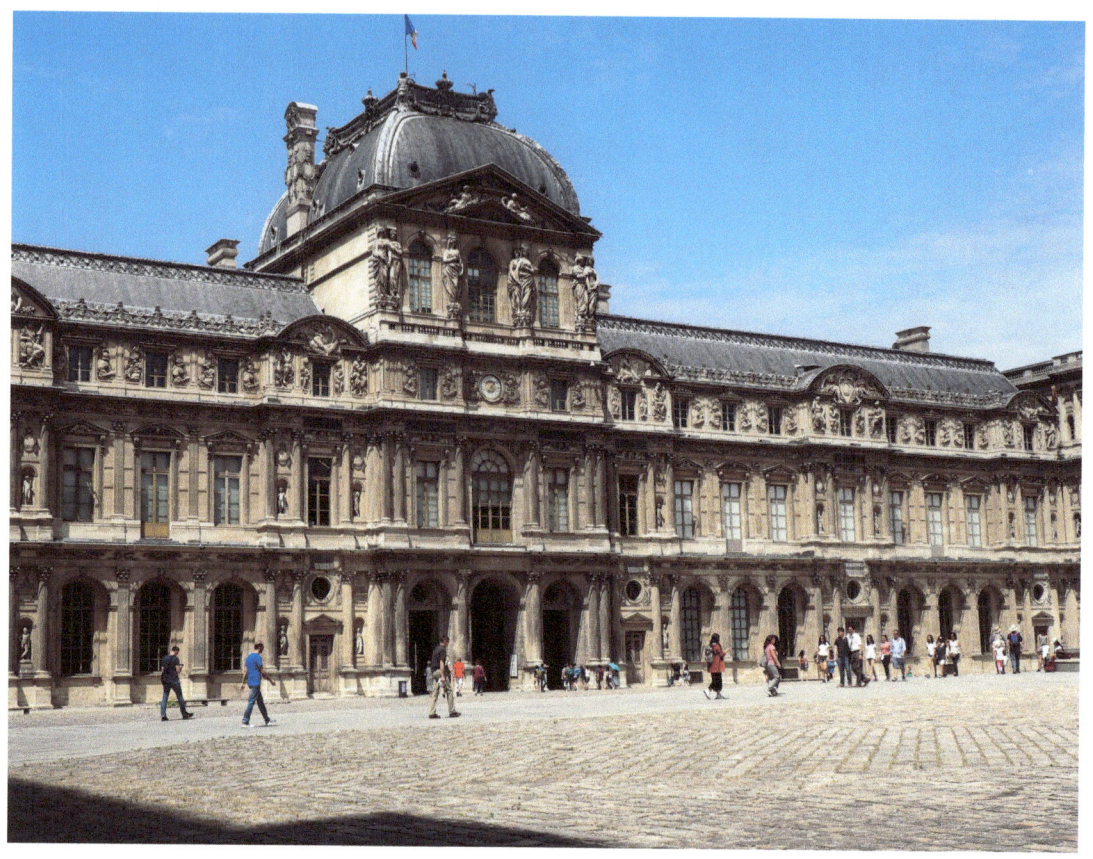

There was an energy at the Louvre that water couldn't quench, maybe wine or coffee could have quenched it. But I had neither. A very different energy than our Carnival Tuesday, quenched by rum and Carib, soca and feathers, prayers and church camps.

When I sat in the courtyard of the Louvre, the crows in the distance captured the sombre energy, despite the constant chatter of the tourists.

The stone walls were carpeted by a cobblestoned courtyard that grew bits of dry weeds between the neatly arranged stones. These wild weeds blew in the subtle wind, a reminder of life and death and history. Of all who sacrificed themselves in the name of "Liberté, égalité, fraternité" The national motto of France.

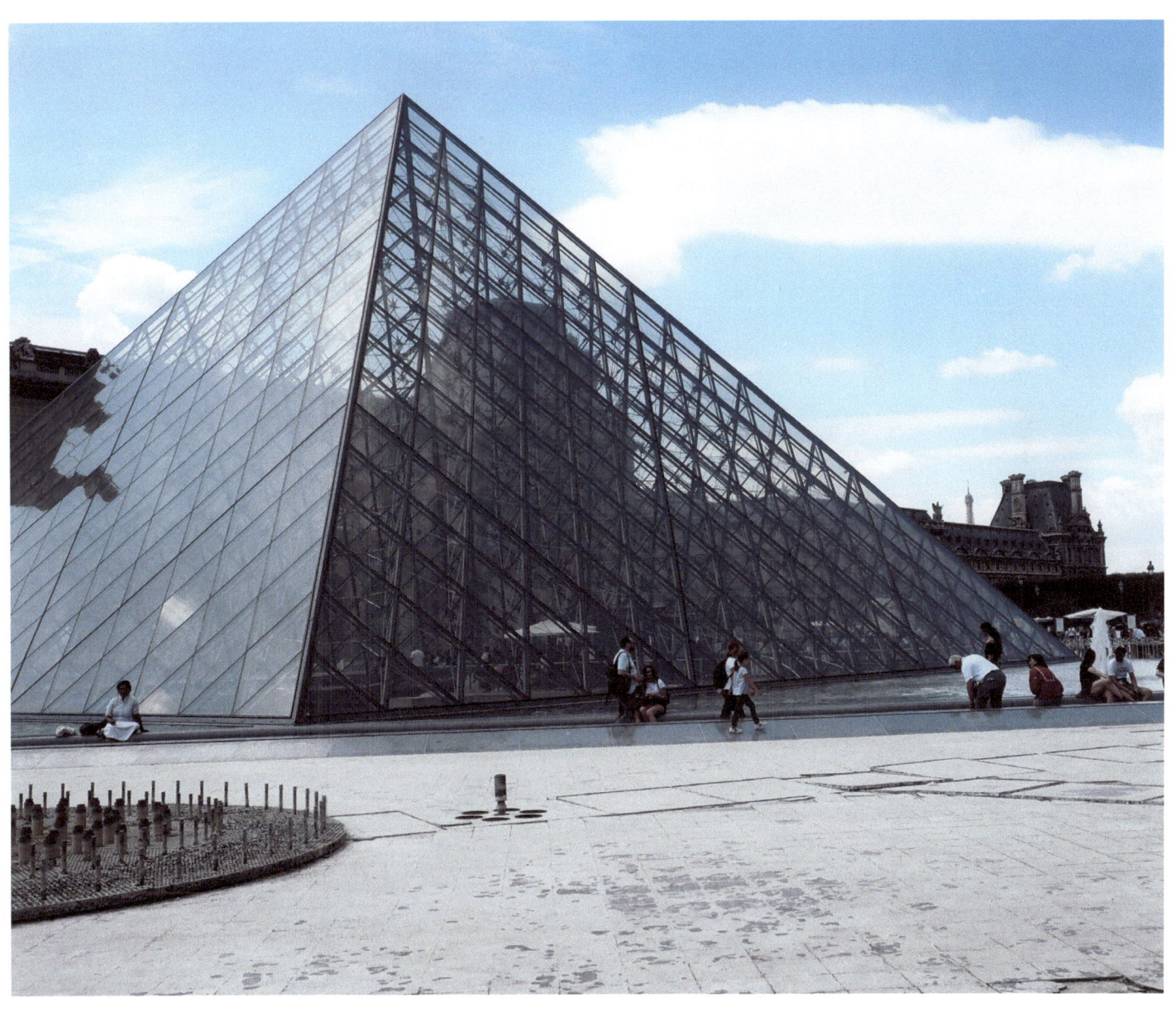

I have noticed that people are so busy with their cameras and phones and camcorders, that they don't stop and admire anything anymore, if not through a lens.

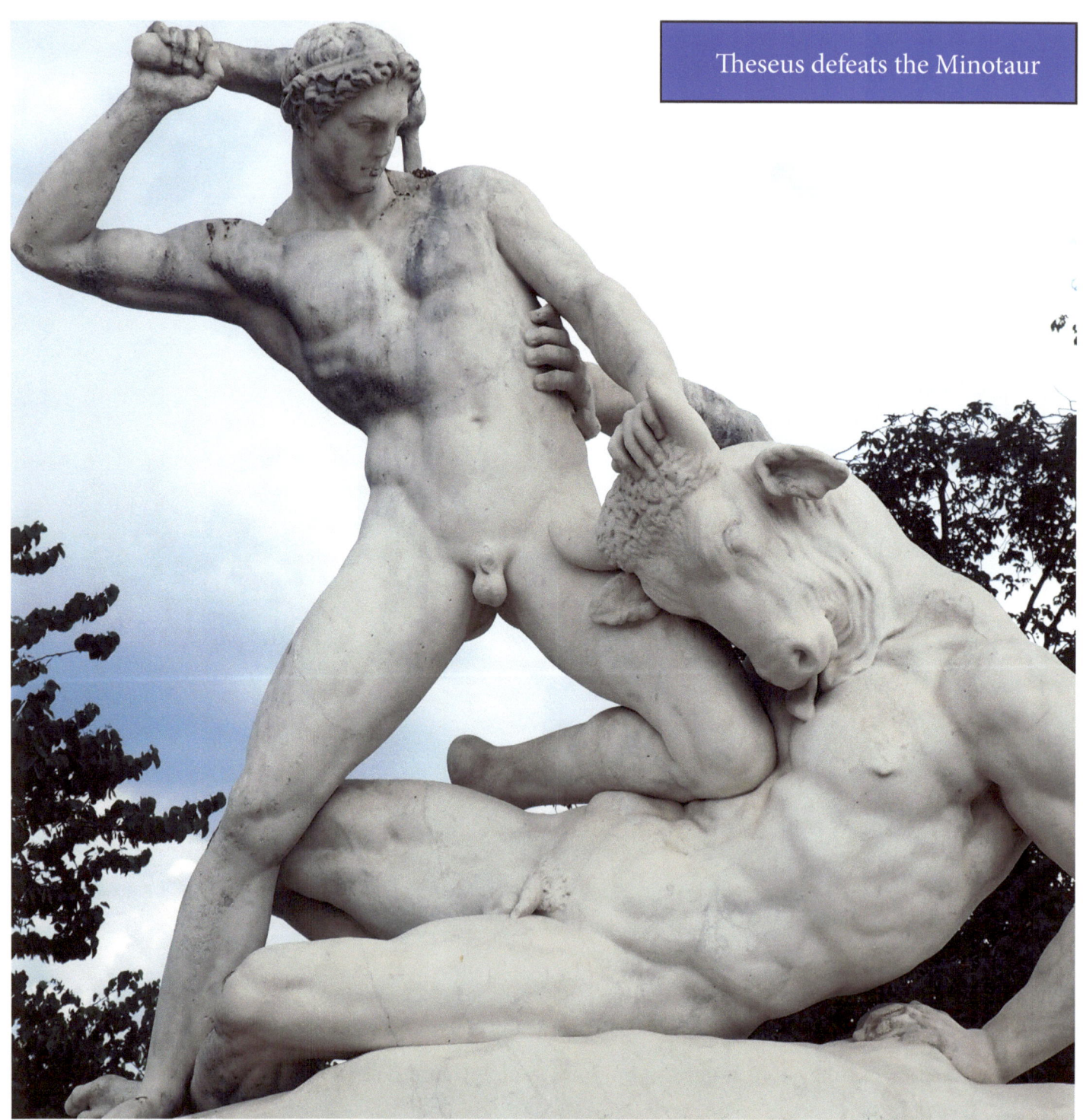

Theseus defeats the Minotaur

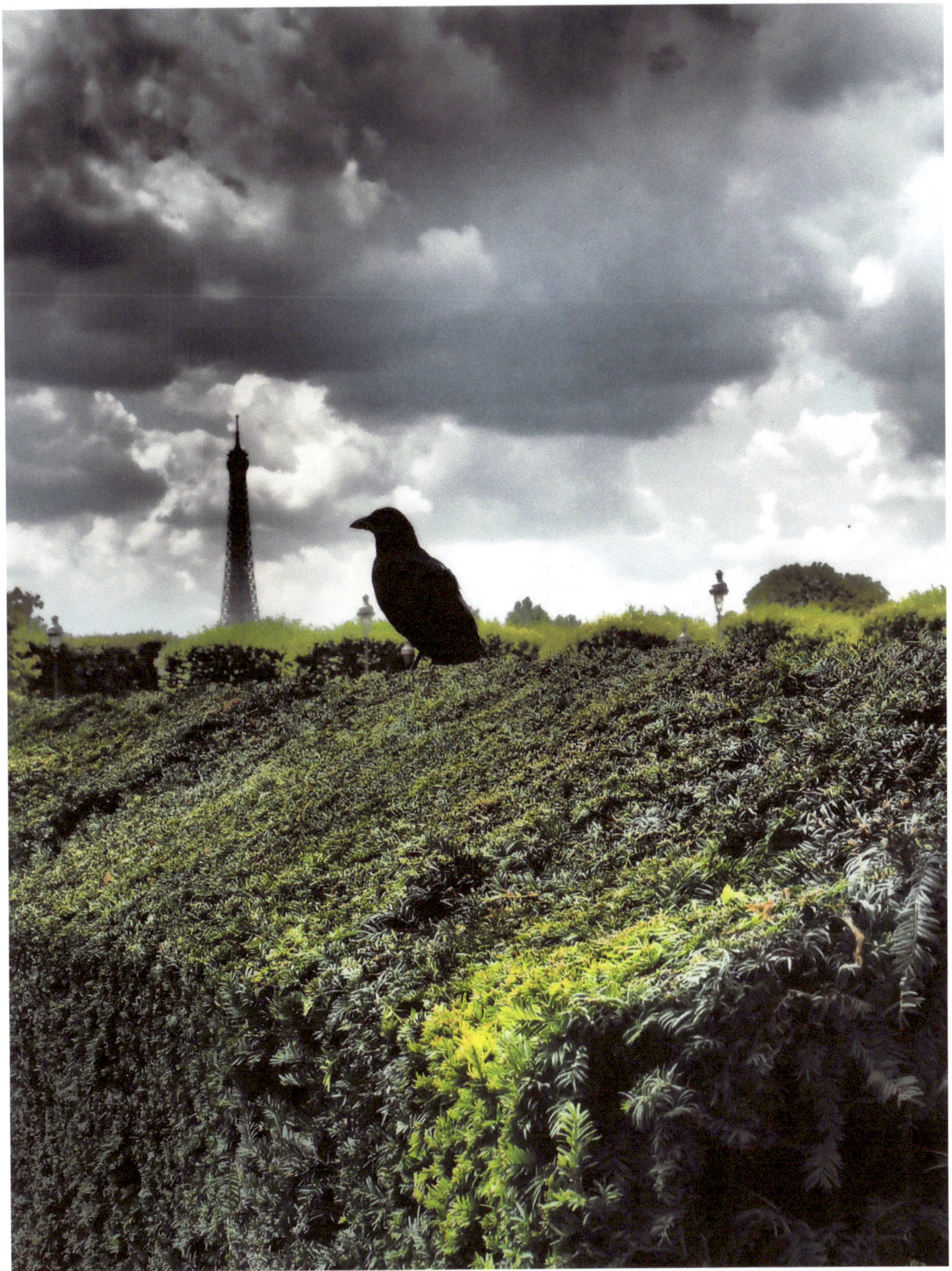

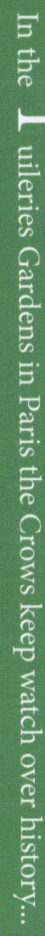

In the Tuileries Gardens in Paris the Crows keep watch over history...

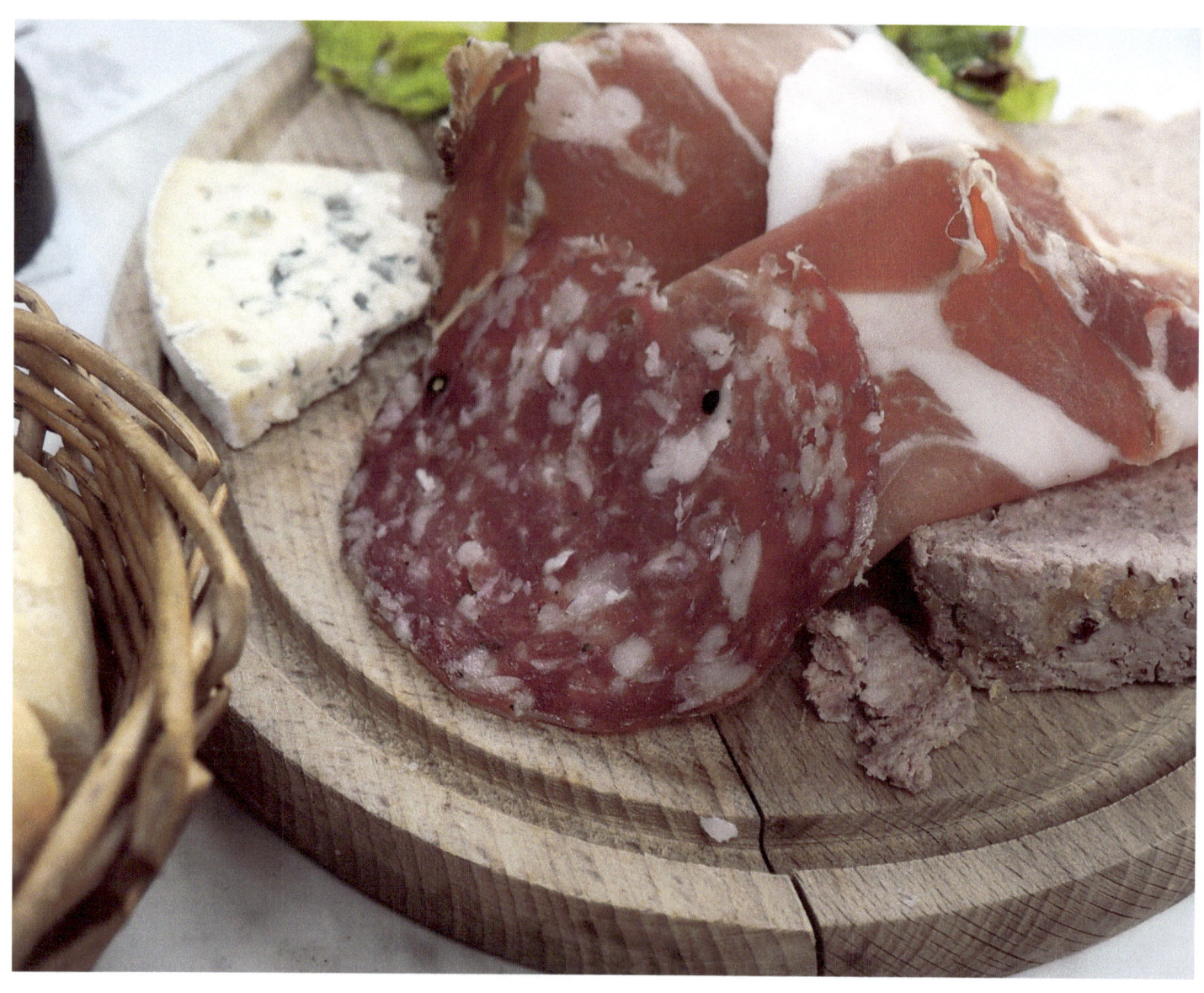

On our walk back to the hotel, we stopped for an afternoon snack at a cafe in Paris.

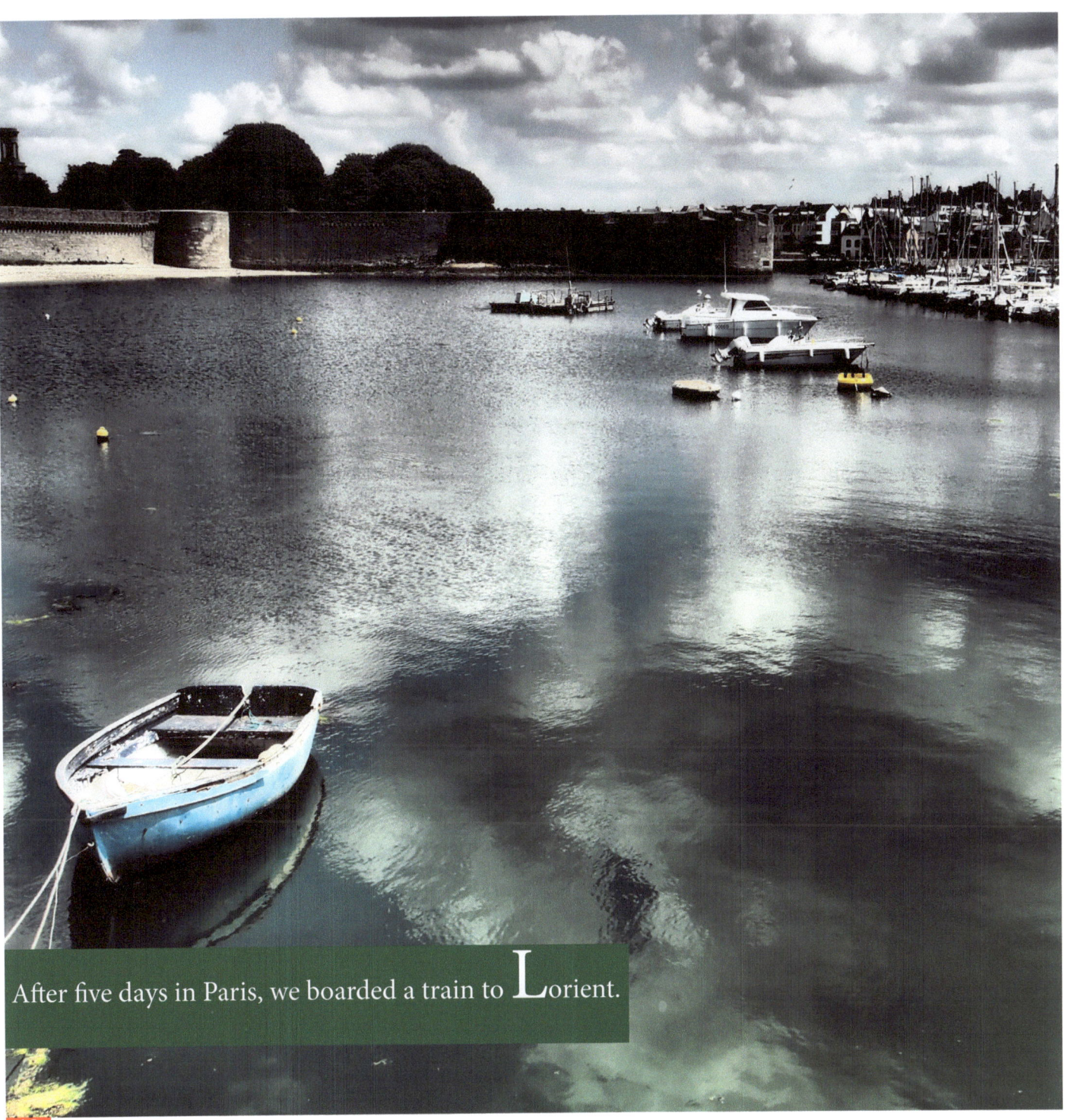

After five days in Paris, we boarded a train to Lorient.

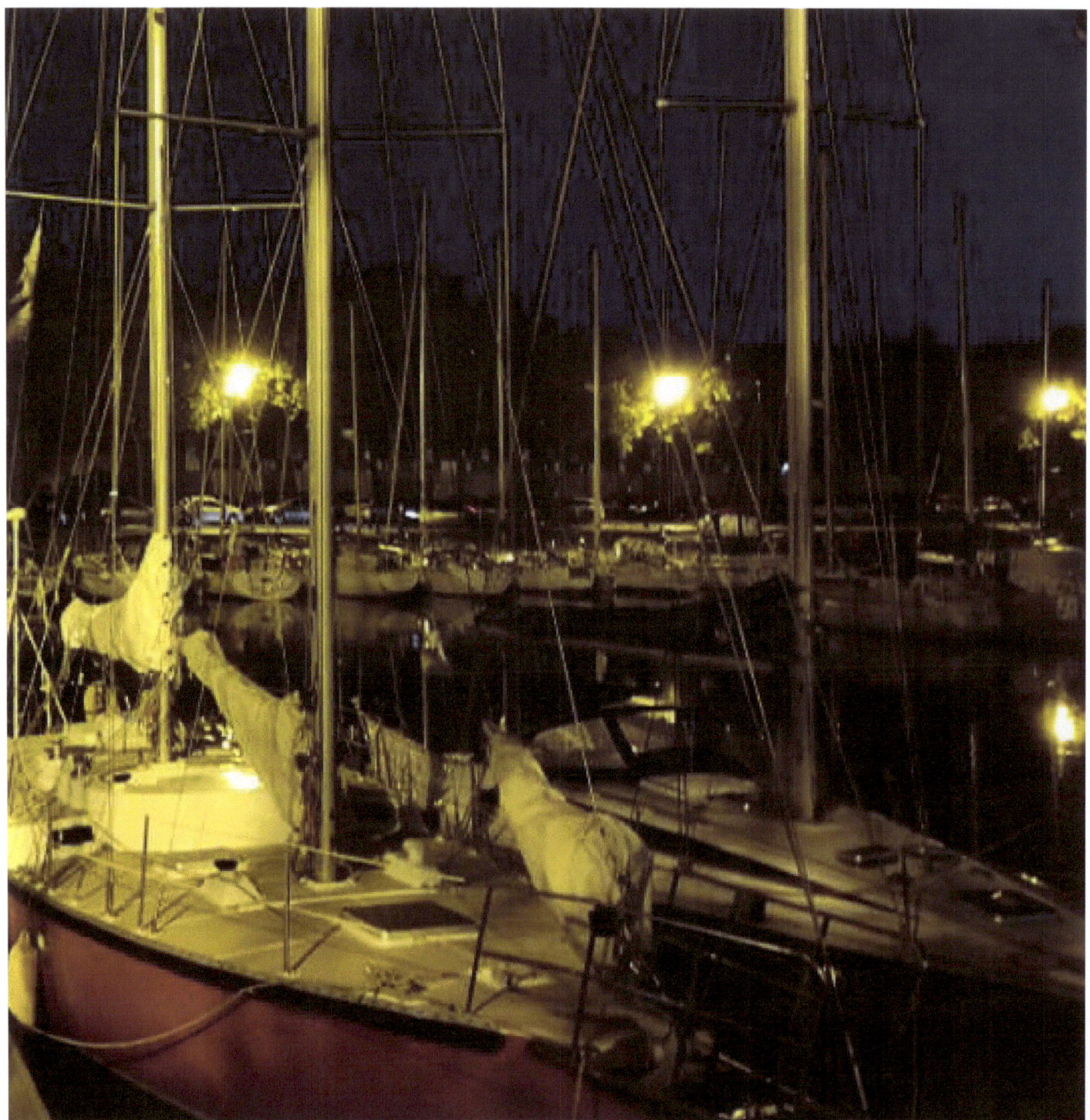

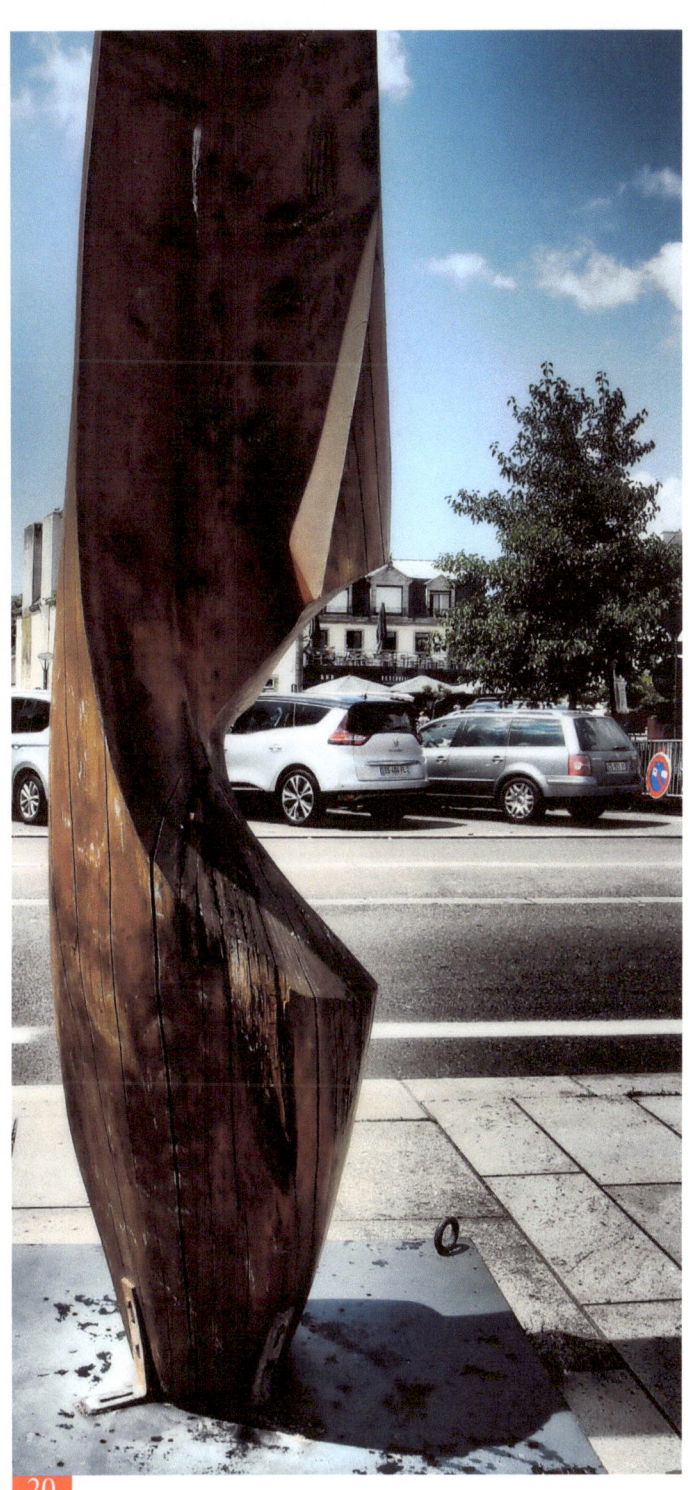

From Lorient we drove to Concarneau, a medieval walledtown in the centre of a harbour. Concarneau is in the Finistère department of Brittany in north-western France, and bordered to the west by the Baie de La Forêt.

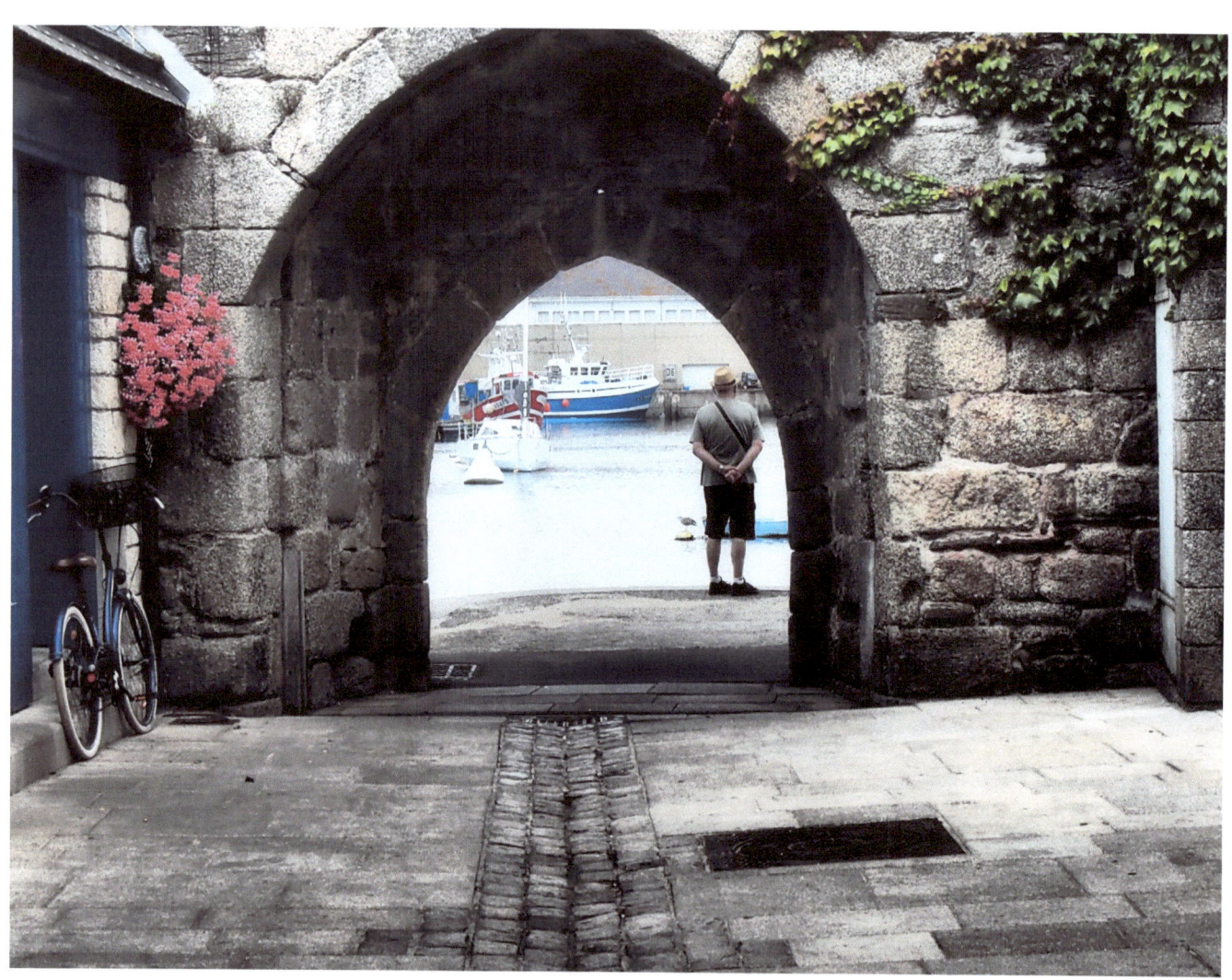

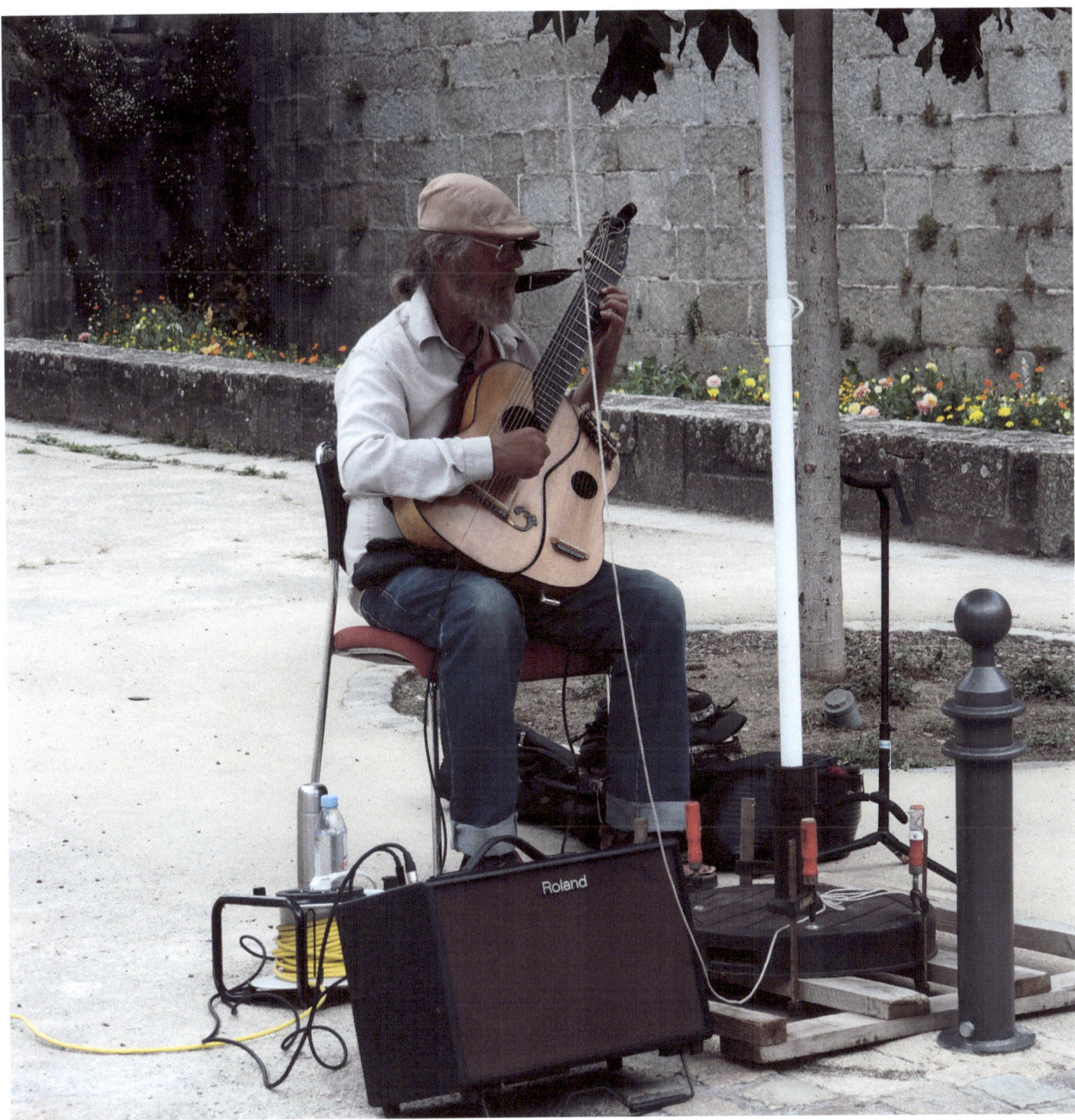

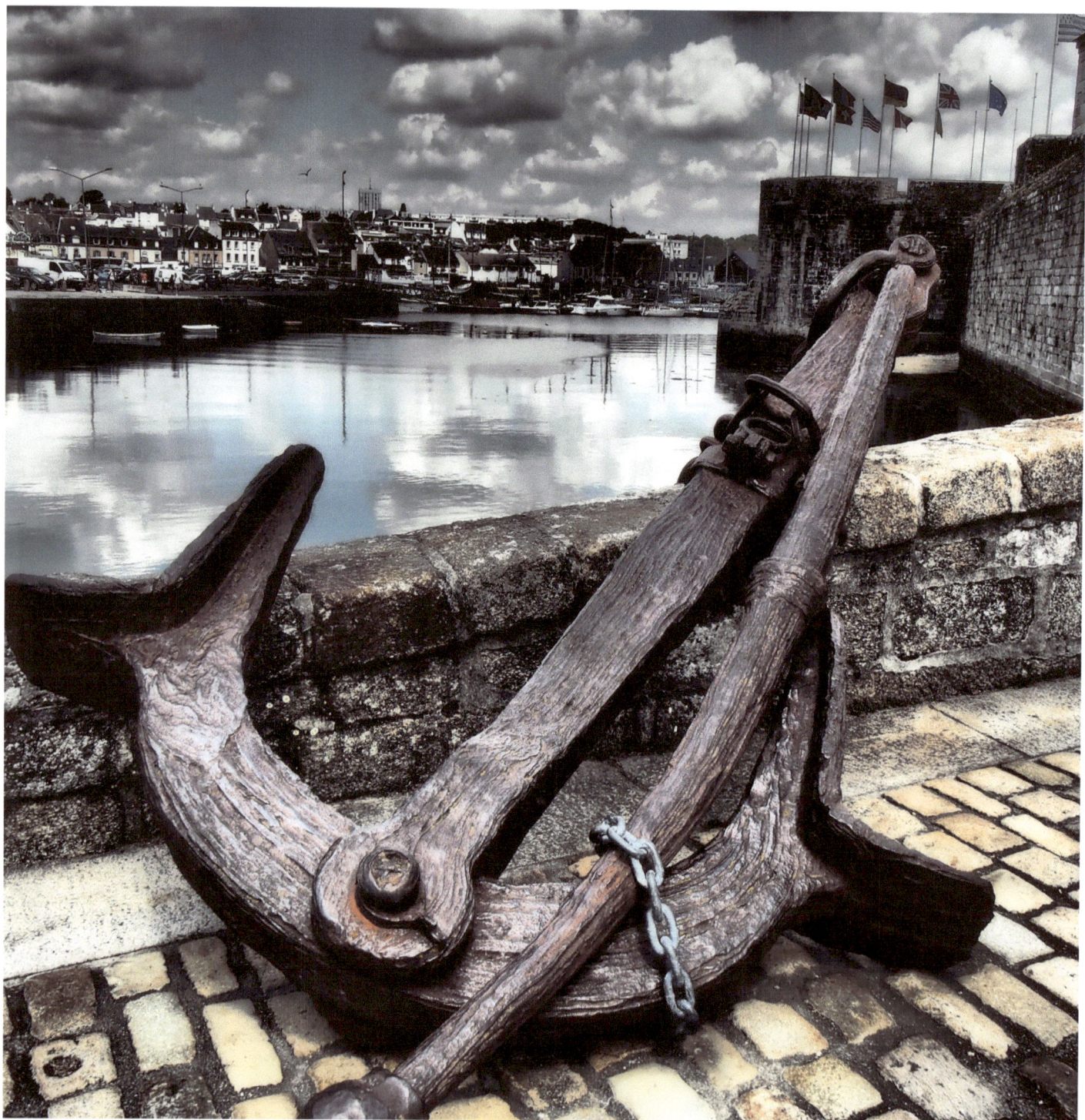

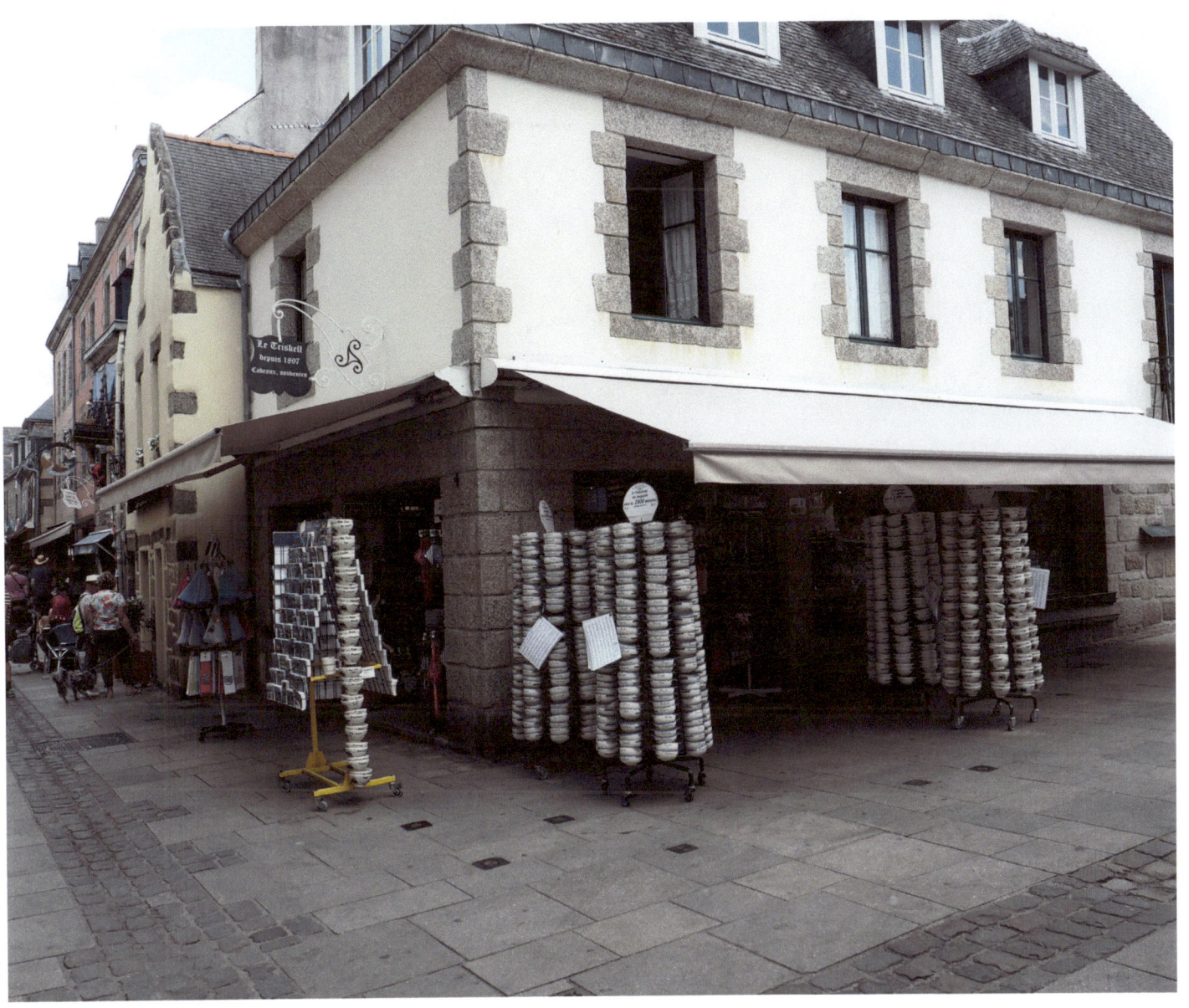

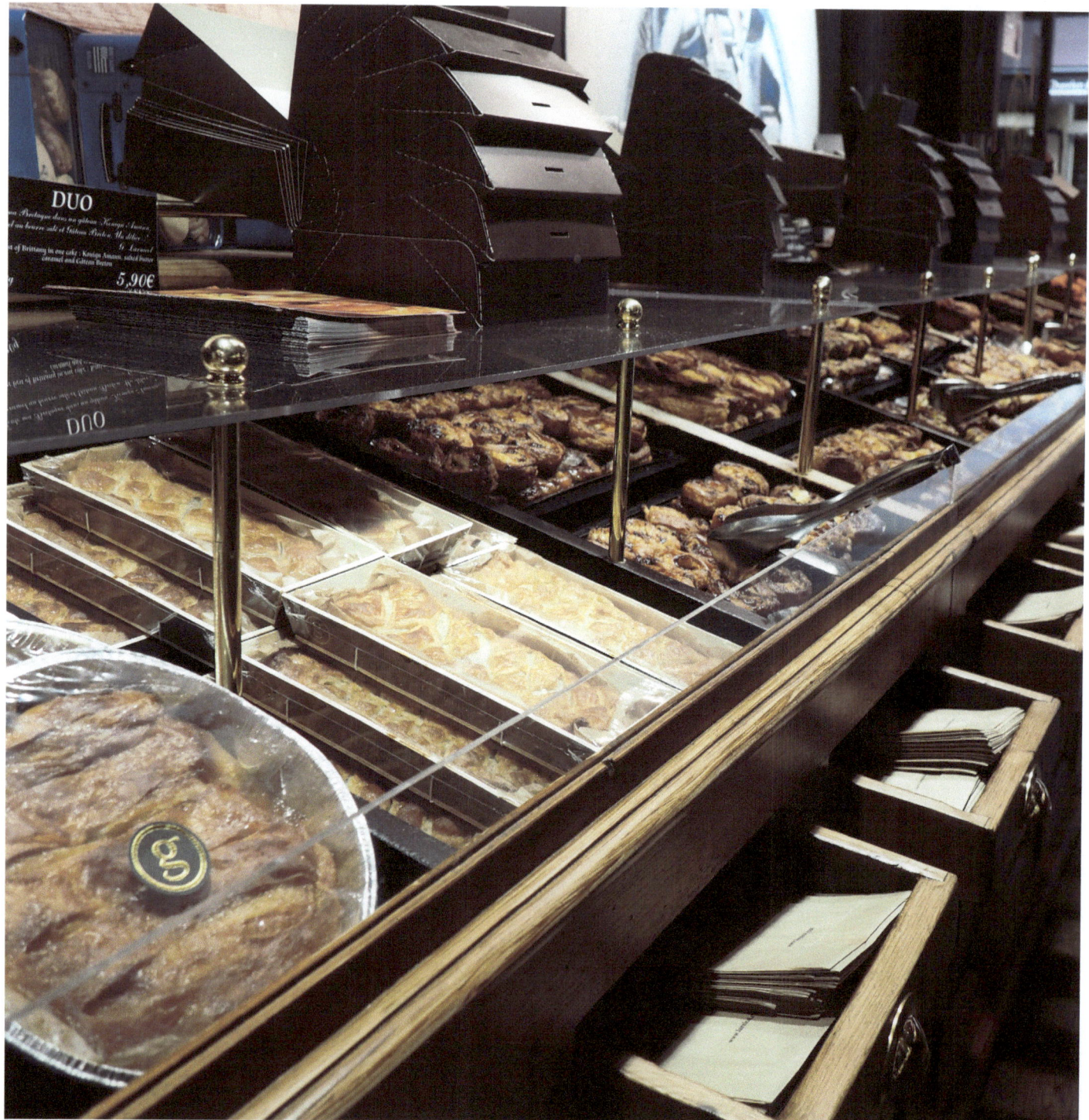

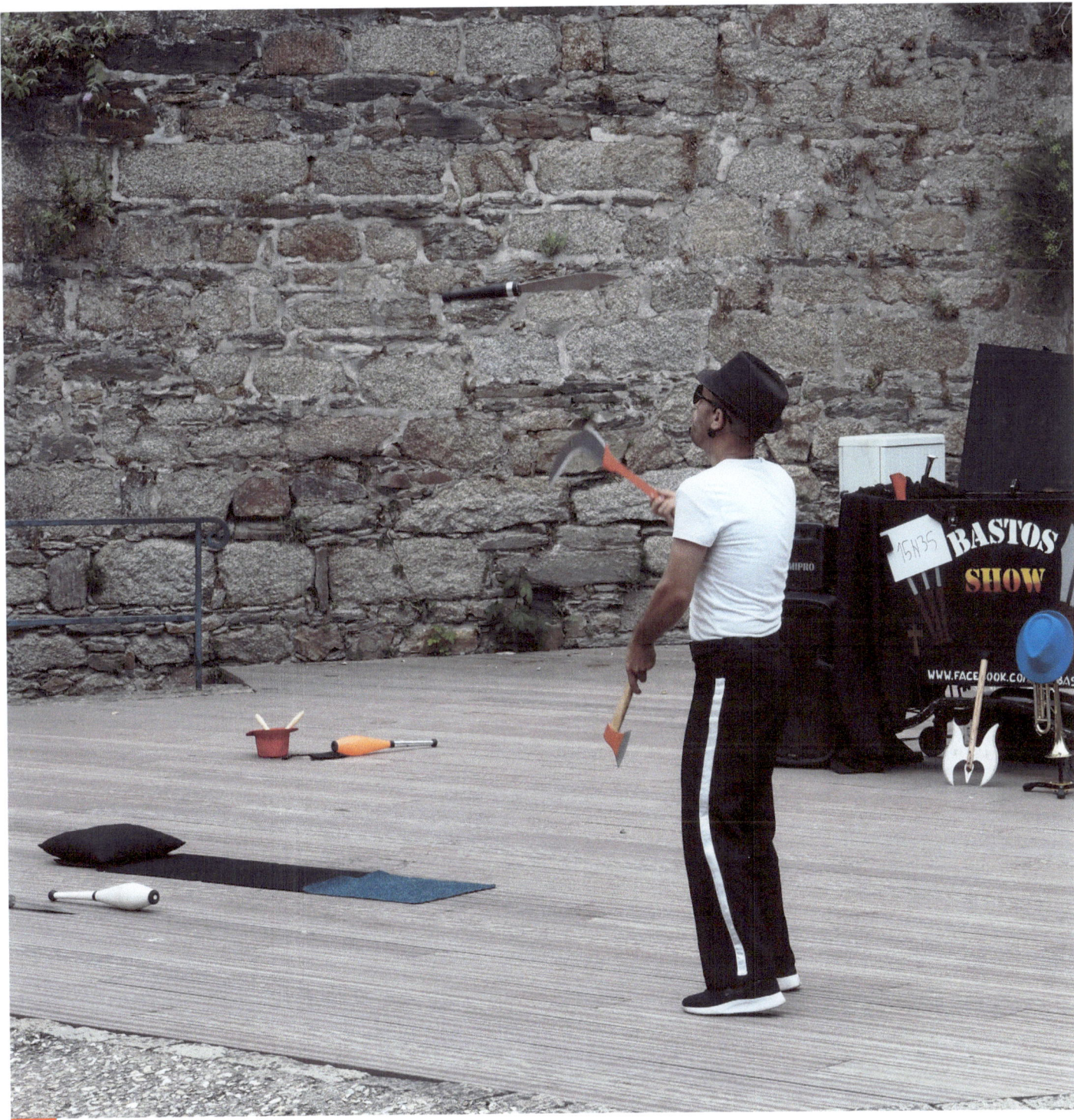

Kindred spirits...artists will always find ways of communicating

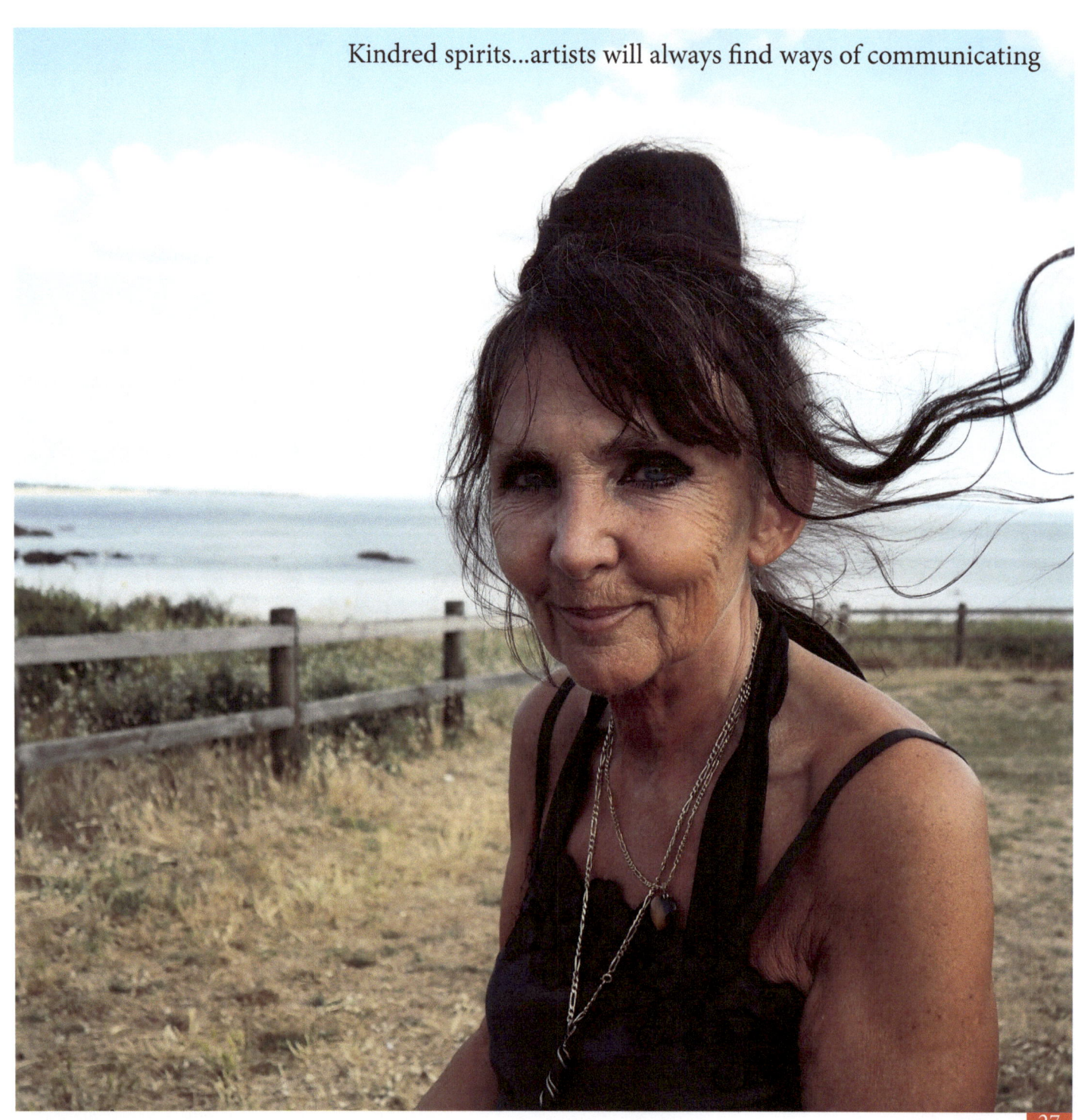

The Pyrenees

The Basque people inhabited the foothills of the Pyrenees Mountains around the Bay of Biscay in northern Spain and southern France for thousands of years. They are the oldest surviving ethnic group in Europe.

Once you enter the town, the similarities of the houses catch your attention. Big and small stone houses plastered white, with red roofs and wooded shutters. At the side of each exterior wall, the original colour of the stone, protrudes slightly to create an interlocking pattern. Old buildings with stories that predate many of us stare at the mountains. Green ivy tells secrets to the white walls as it inches itself up the sides of these plastered houses.

The lush and majestic mountains are not only breathtaking, but meditative. Every year, hundreds of people take the month long pilgrimage up and over the Pyrenees to Spain. You see them with backpacks, in pairs, small groups, solo travellers, on bikes, on feet, all on their own private journey.

We drove up, and not even at its highest peak, there were clouds around us, with a still atmosphere that silenced our thoughts, till we were stripped of ego and doubts and hang-ups. Until it is just you and this divine essence that people call by so many names……..

A Road trip

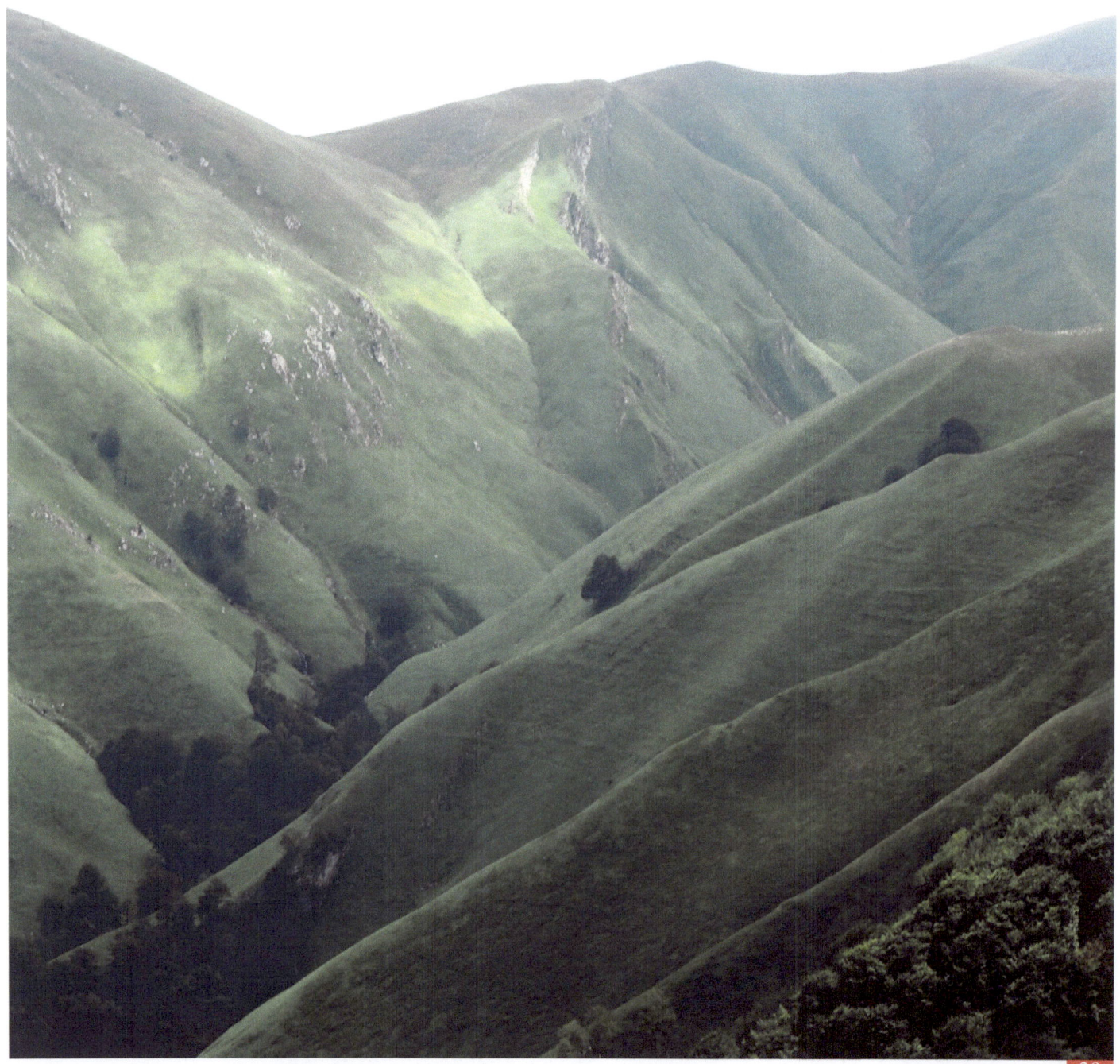

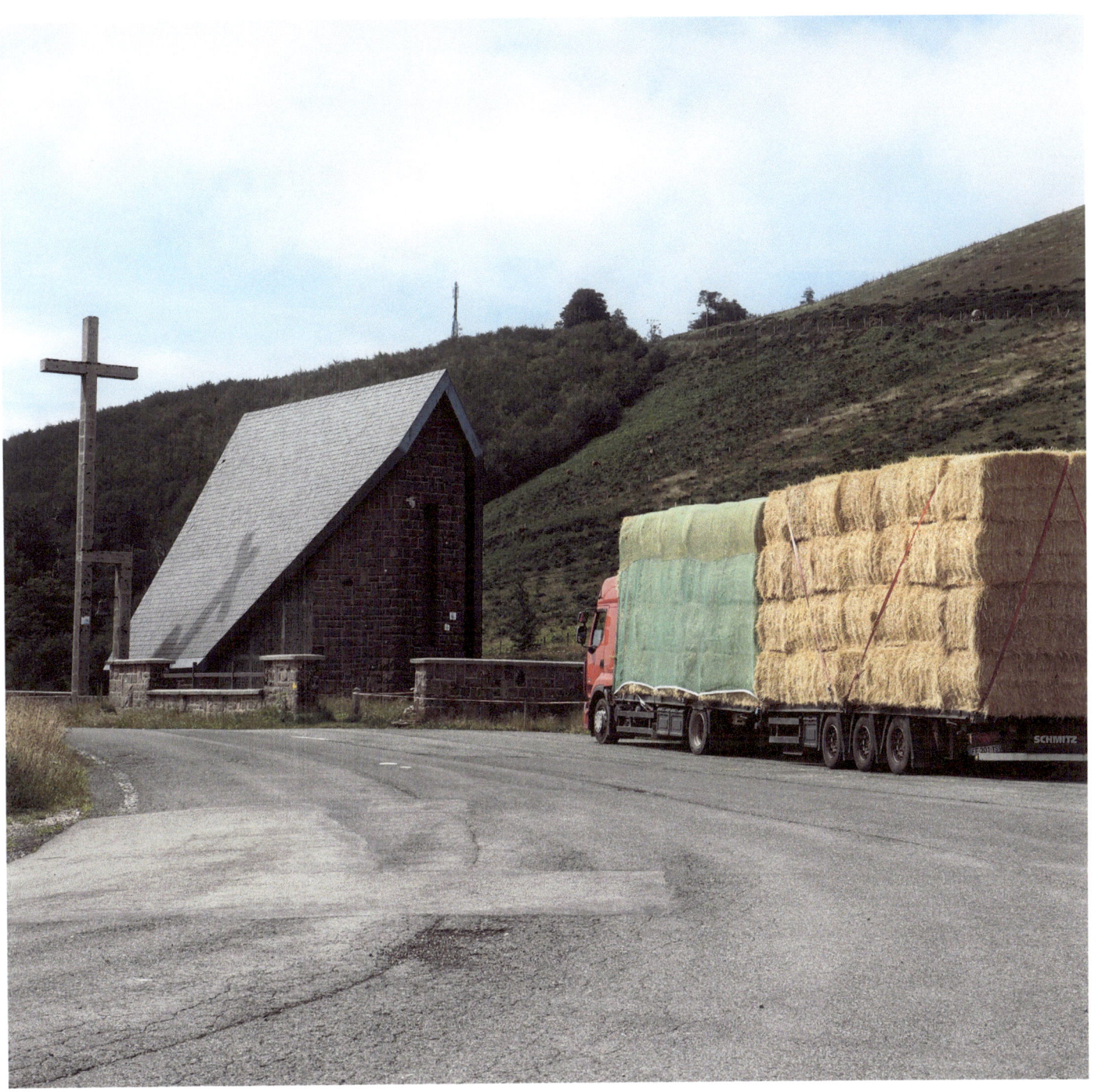

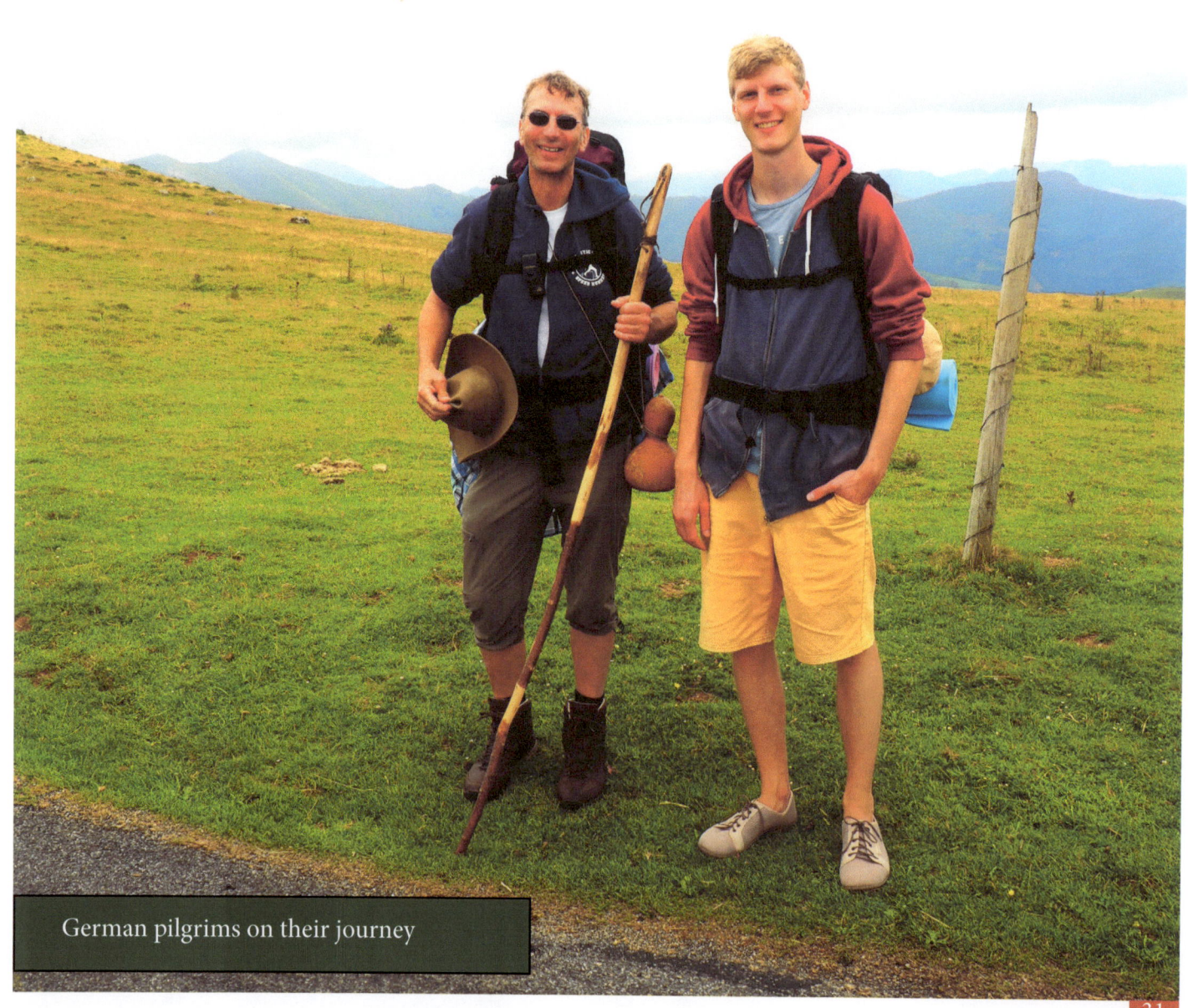
German pilgrims on their journey

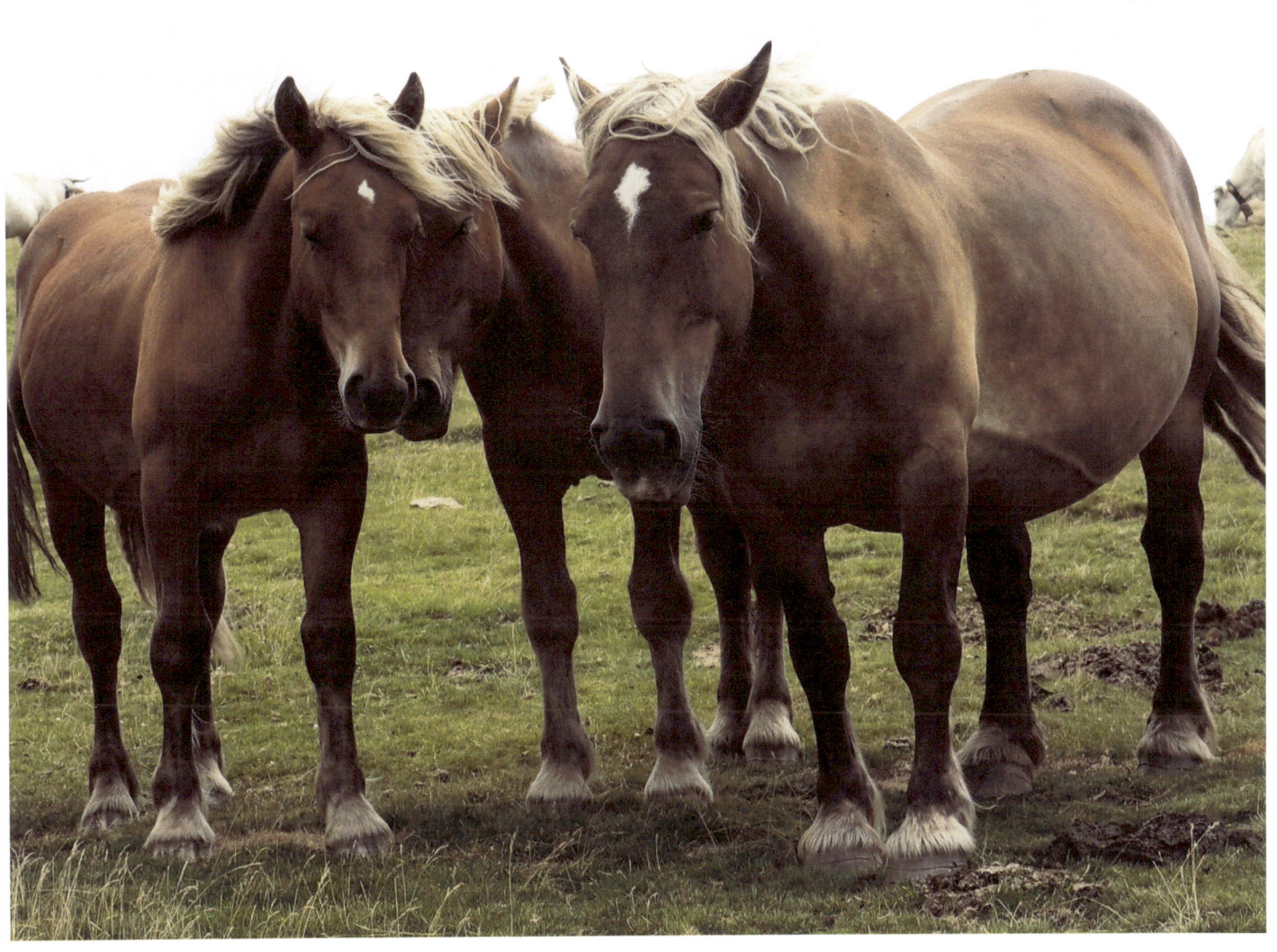

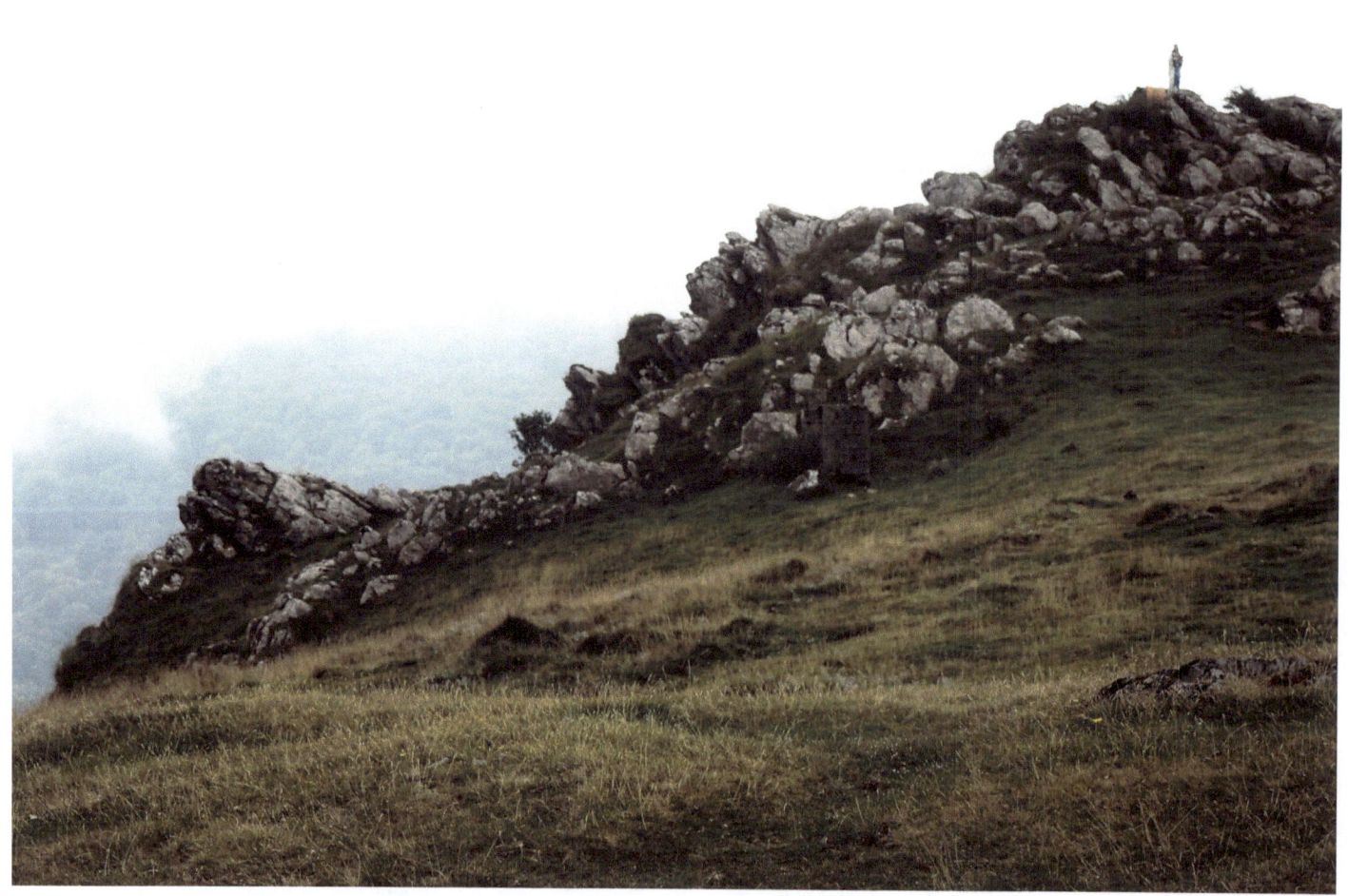

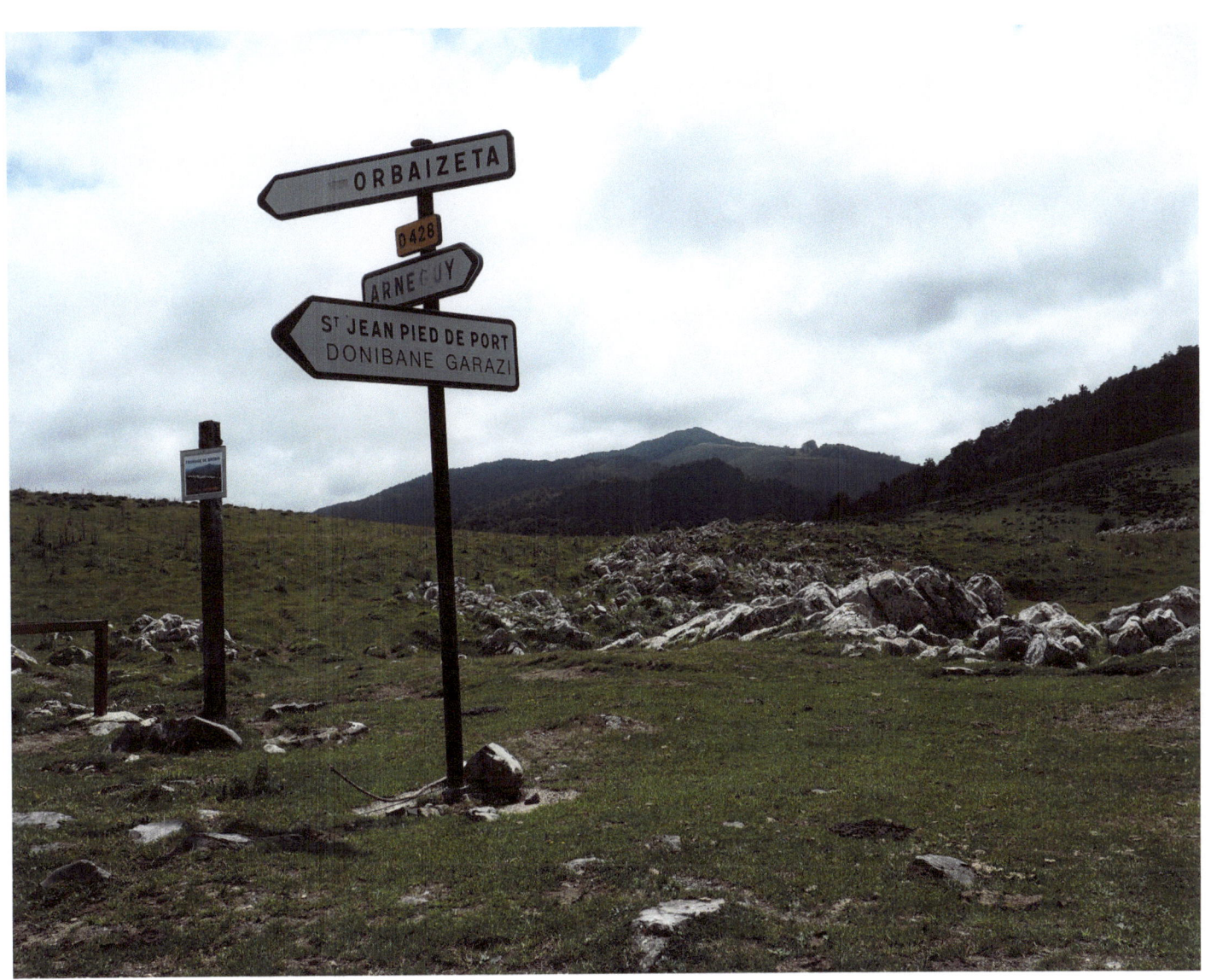

Life is filled with cross roads, offering many choices....

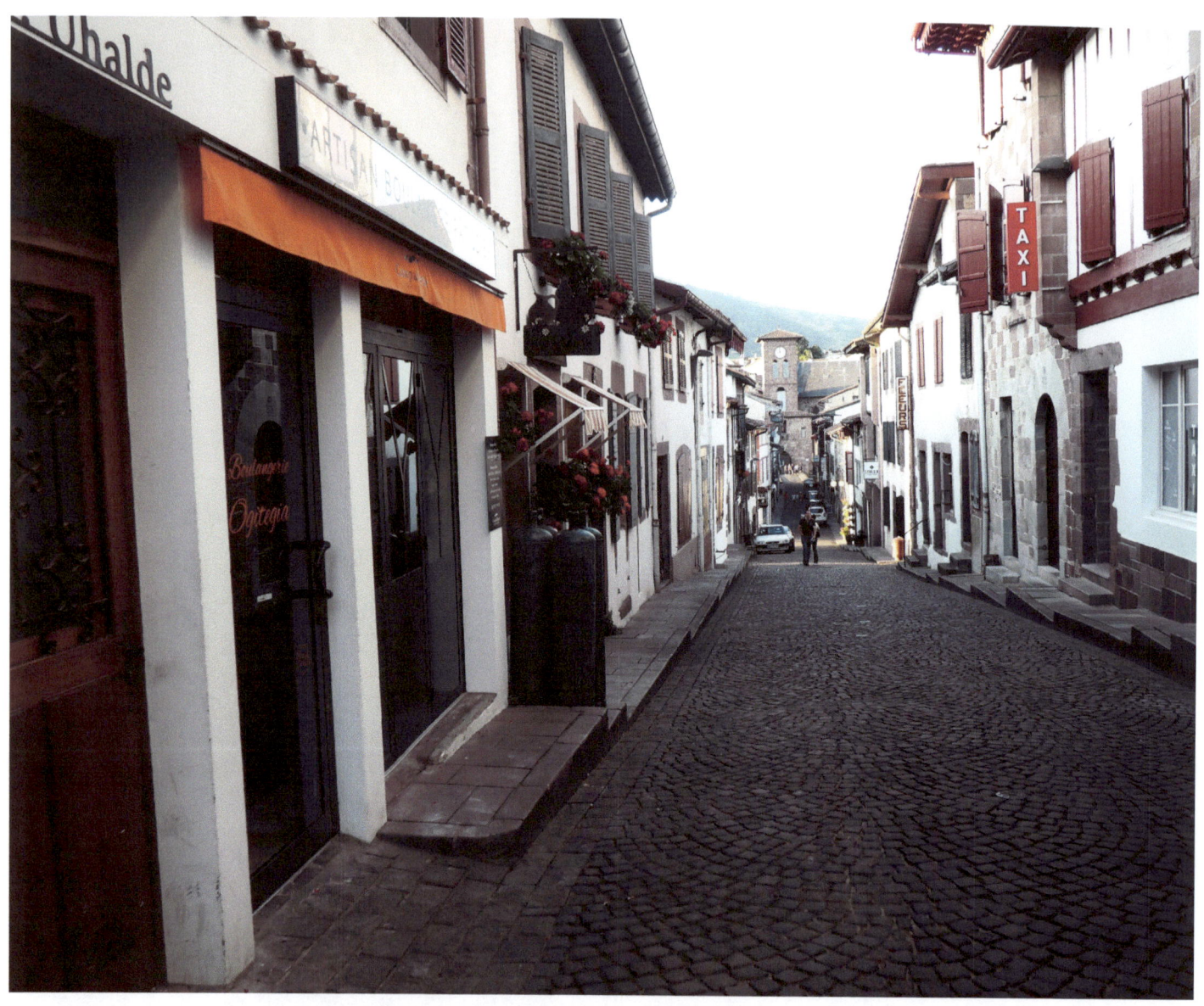

When we visited the Pyrenees, we stayed in the town of St Jean Pied de Port, an old but very historically rich town. Filled with tradition.

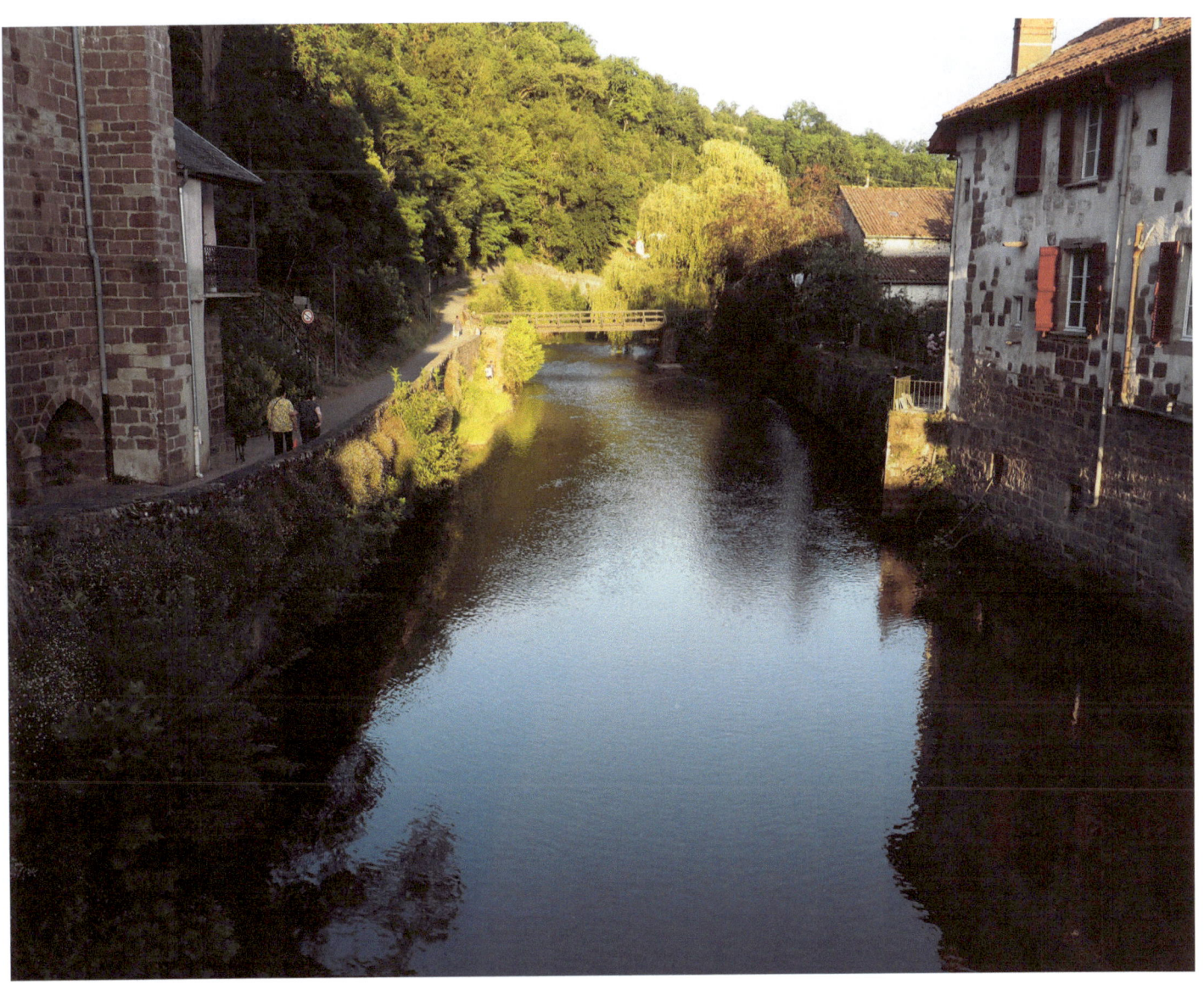

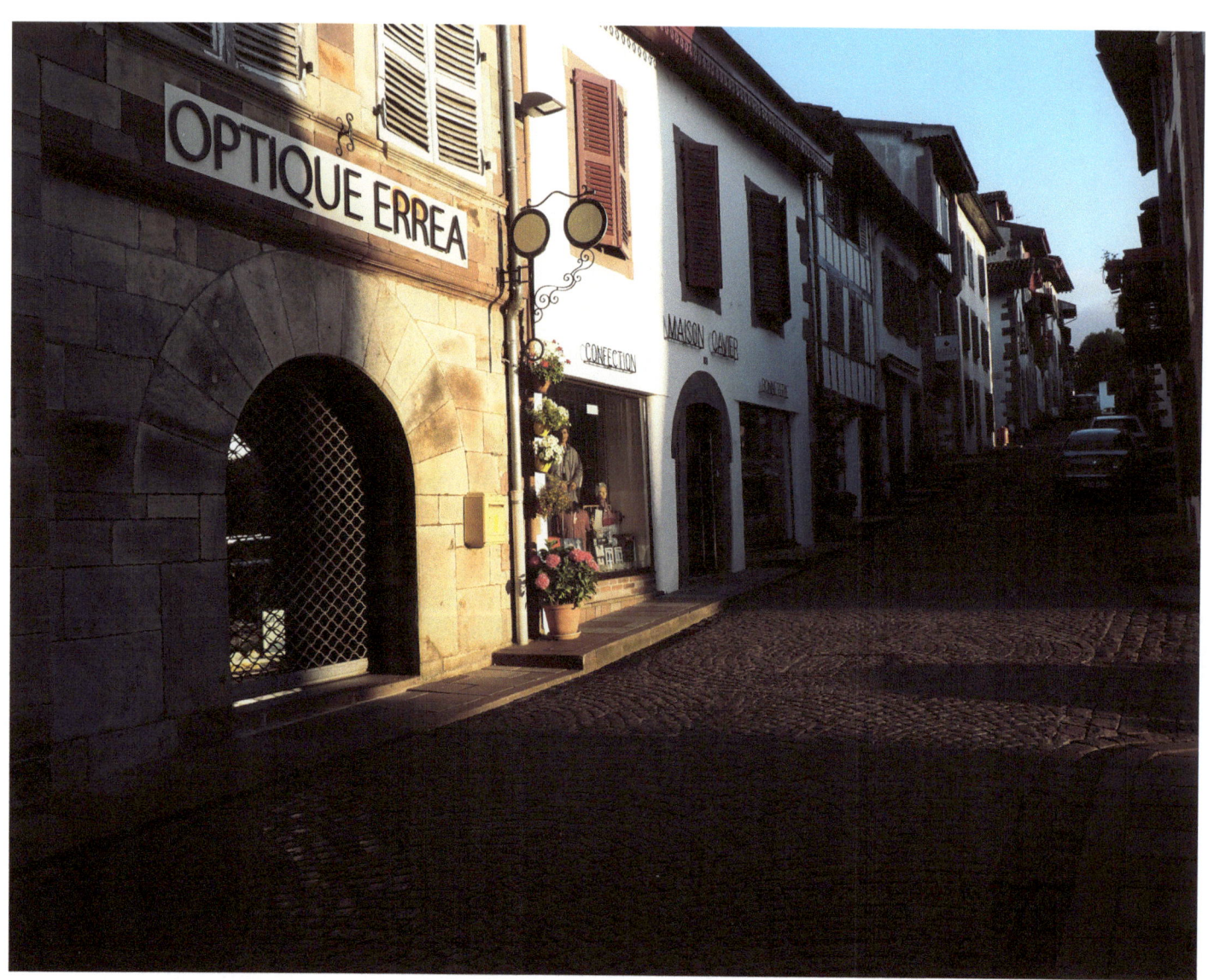

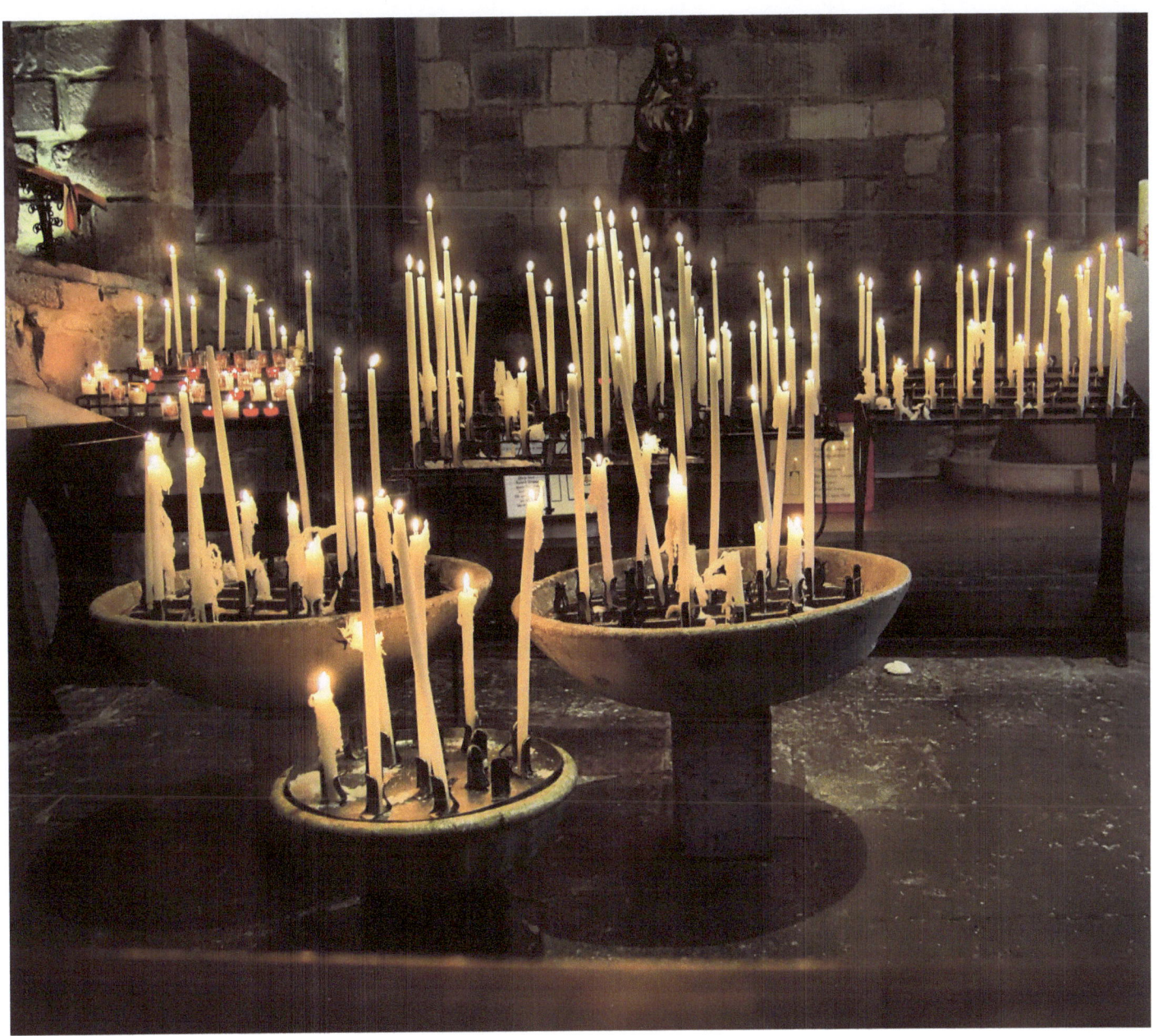

PORTE NOTRE-DAME
Access to the Faubourg d'Espagne

The Notre-Dame gateway is the best preserved of those providing access to the town of Saint-Jean-Pied-de-Port, and still retains vestiges of its former monumental studded doors and original portcullis. This gateway leads to the Faubourg d'Espagne, a new medieval district wich was particulaly developed beyond the surrounding walls in the 17th and 18th centuries. On the other side of the bridge spanning the river Nive, the rue d'Espagne was a thriving quarter with numerous merchants and craftsmen. Cobblers, weavers, goldsmiths, stone-cutters and chocolate makers, among others, proudly exposed their wares on the market stalls, attracting custom from across the entire Pays de Cize. In the mid-18th century the town was comprised of 64 master craftsmen, and 36 compagnons, or assistants. During the same period, a garrison of over 500 men was stationed in the city.

▶ EXQUISITE LINTELS
On either side of the Notre-Dame gateway, in rue de la Citadelle and rue d'Espagne, a series of fine lintels span the doorways, giving valuable information on the date of construction or renovation, in addition to the proprietor's name and profession.

▶ ACROSS THE RIVER NIVE
In the 14th century, a wooden bridge - which could be raised in the event of danger - spanned the river Nive, connecting the two parts of the town. It was an important link, between the upper and lower sections of Saint-Jean-Pied-de-Port. Up until the 11th century no bridge existed here, resulting in serious problems for pilgrims. A ford, thought to have been located somewhere in the Ugange district, was manned by a series of rather dishonest tollmen who helped the pilgrims cross to the other side. Initialy made of wood, the present bridge of Eyheraberry, wich is called today the "Roman Bridge", was built about 1720.

▶ PORTE NOTRE-DAME – A MEETING-POINT FOR PILGRIMS
The entrance to the hospital - where pilgrims would have been received - was located outside the Porte Notre-Dame. An arched passage above the street and the gate allowed the communication between the church and the hospital. Note the stone seats embedded in the walls on either side. This is where the poorest pilgrims used to sit and wait for the hospital to open in order to receive charity and food.

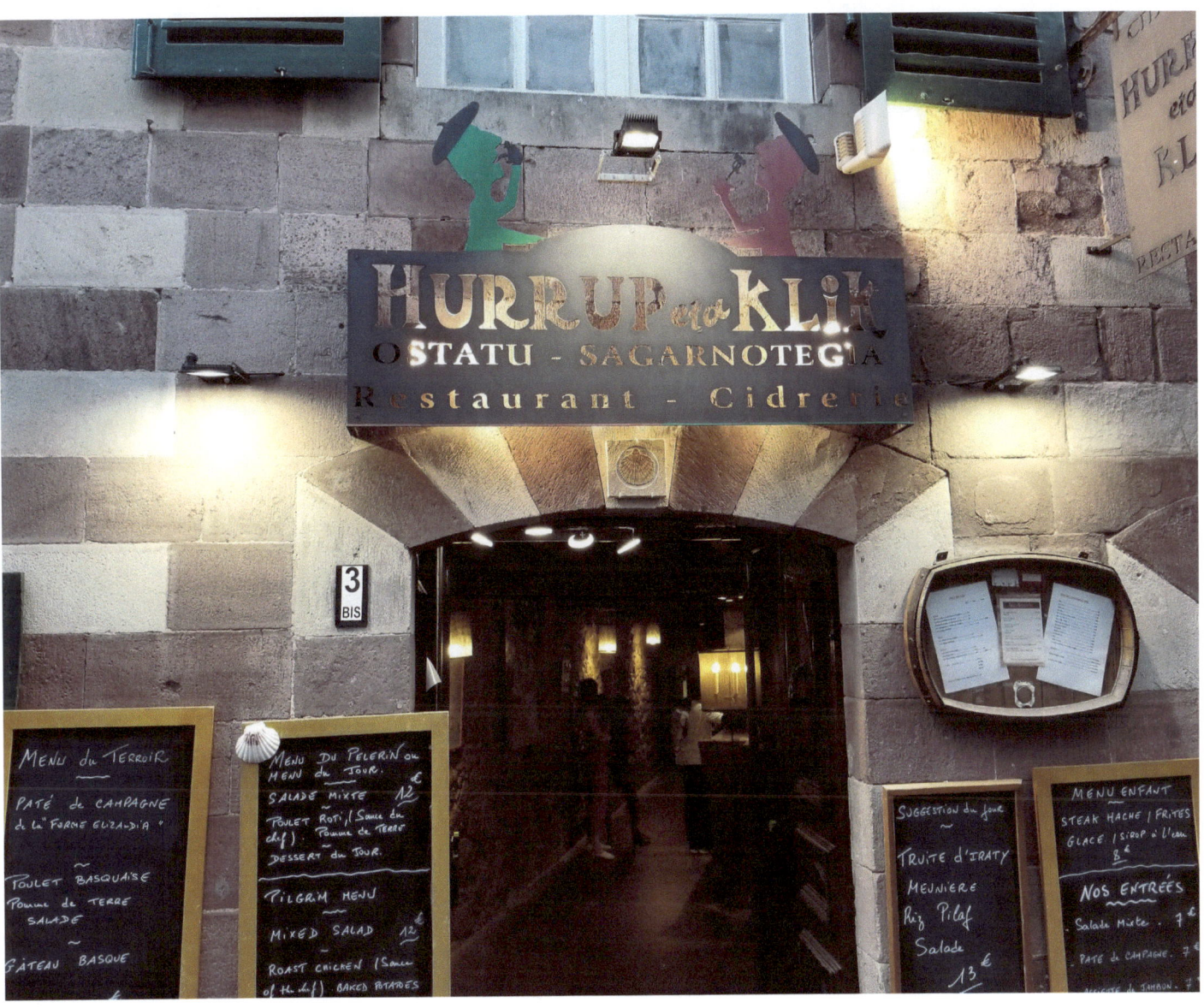

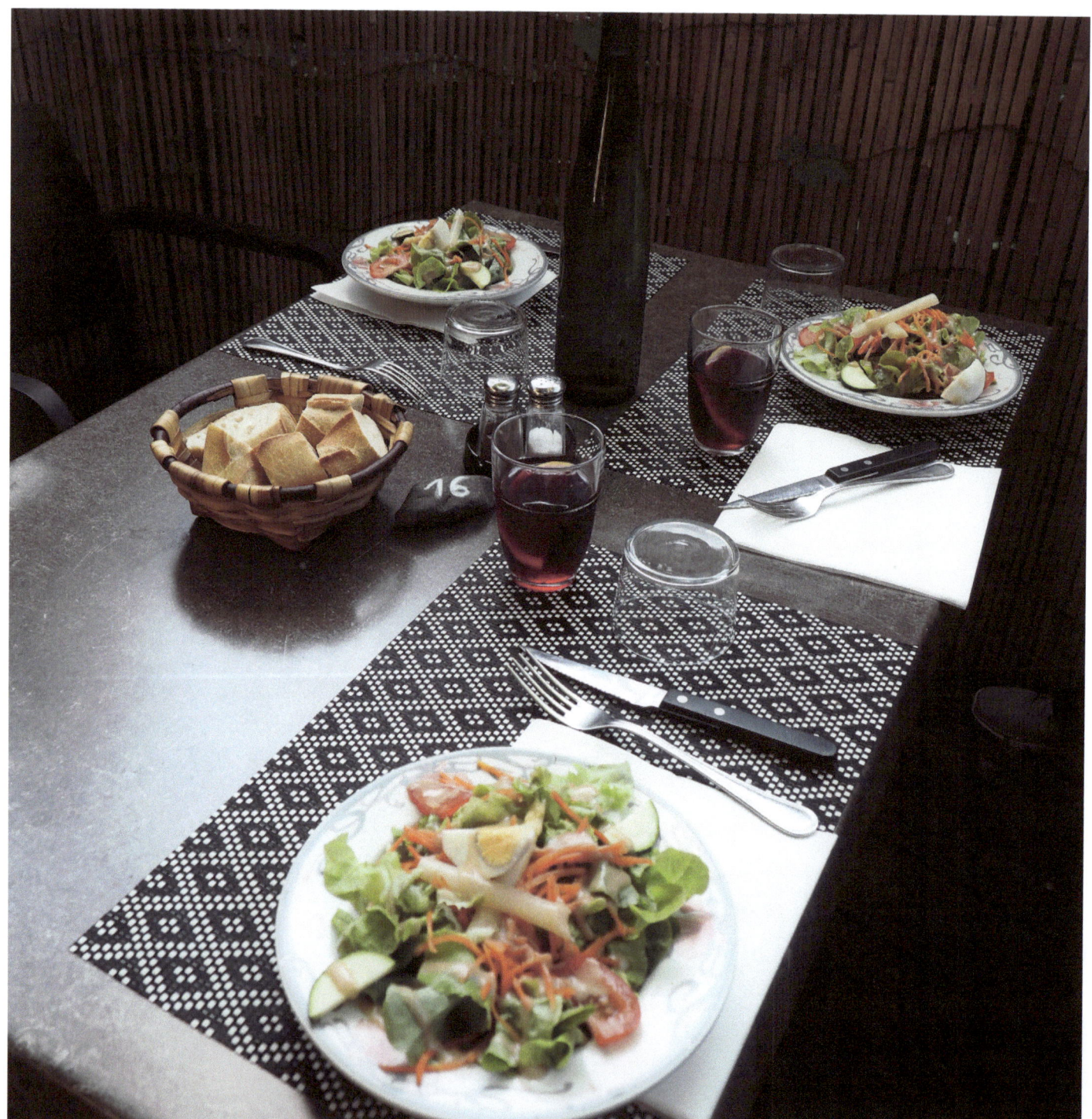

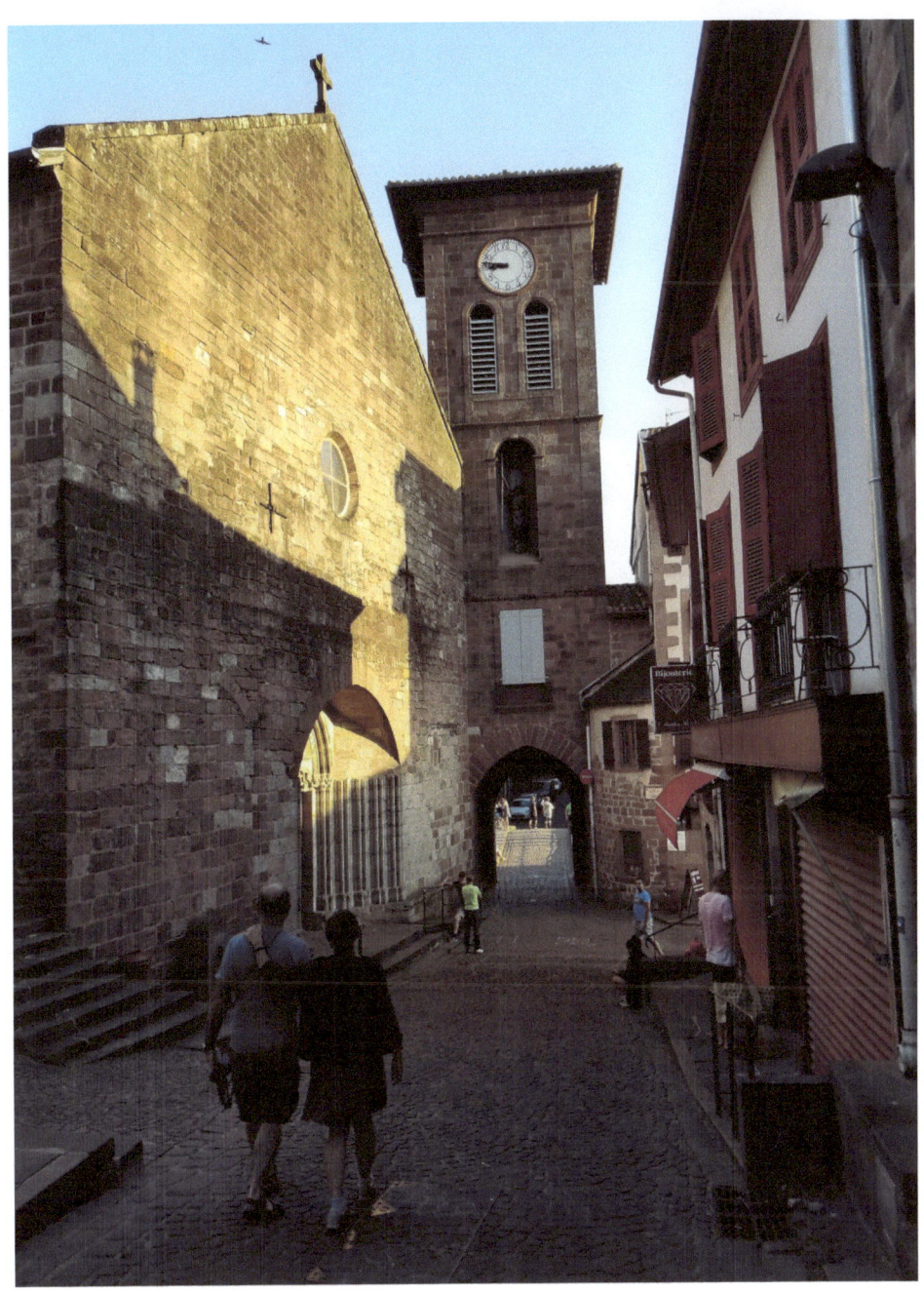

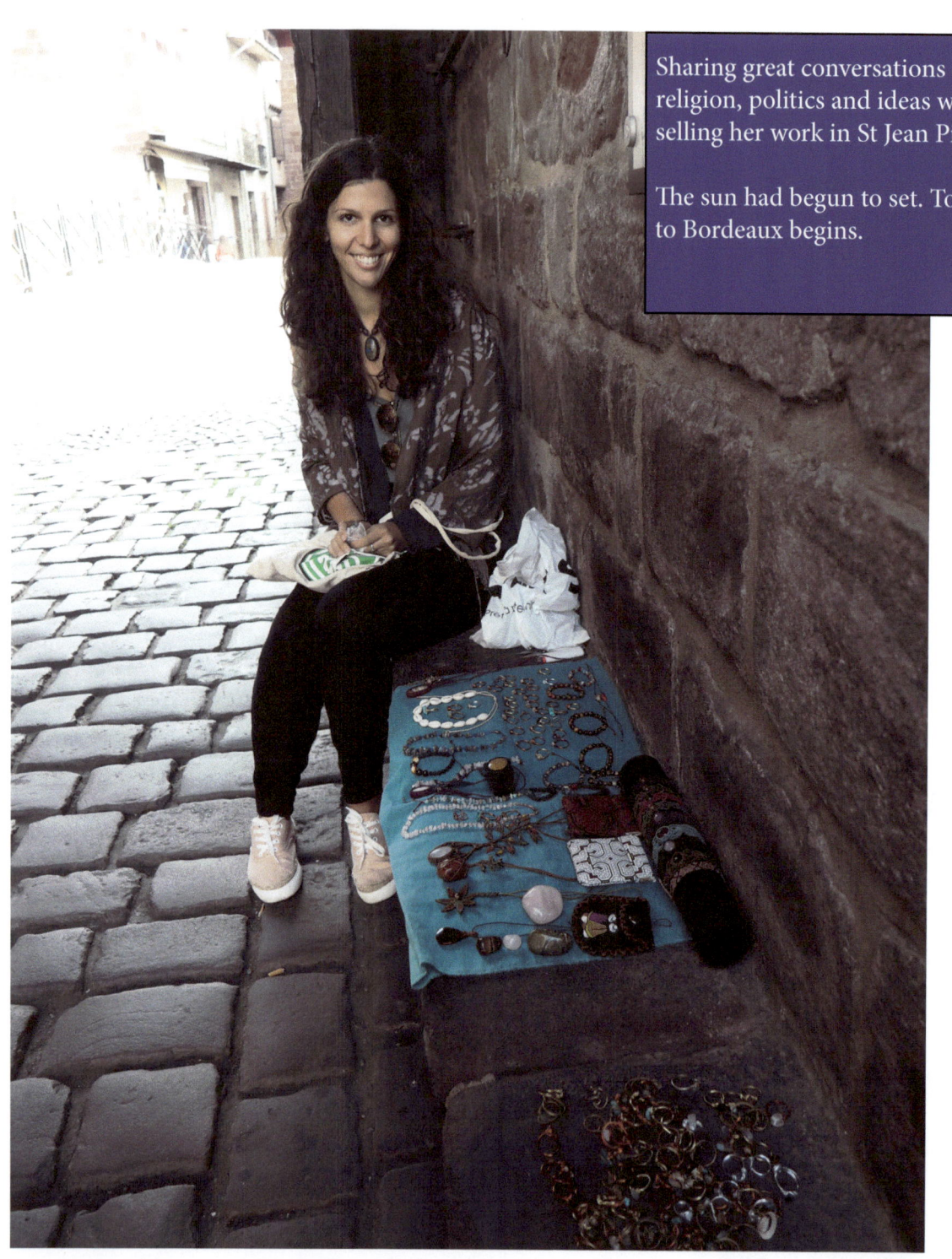

Sharing great conversations on craft work, religion, politics and ideas with a Spanish artist, selling her work in St Jean Pied de Port.

The sun had begun to set. Tomorrow the journey to Bordeaux begins.

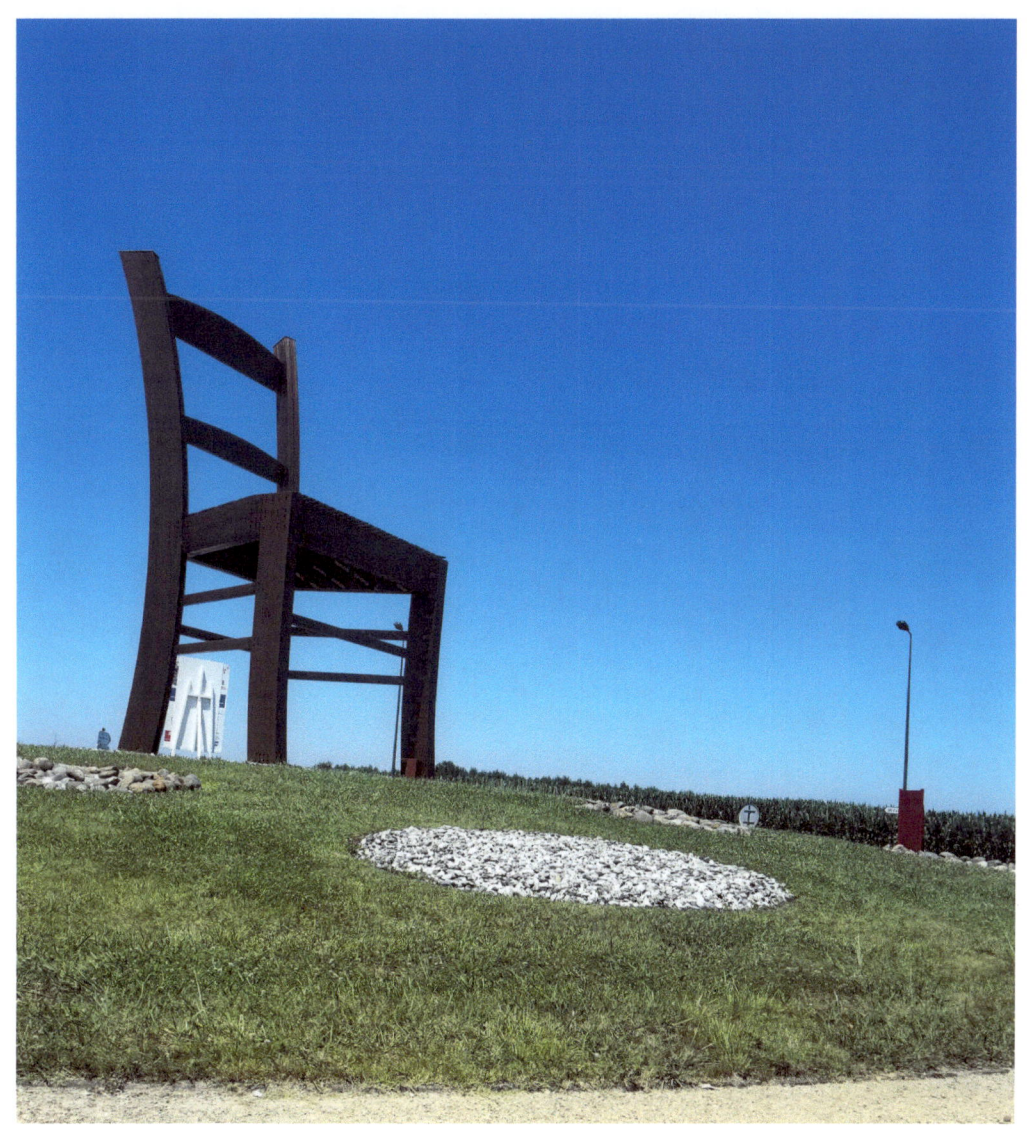

I couldn't help taking a photo of this huge chair at the Hagetmau roundabout.

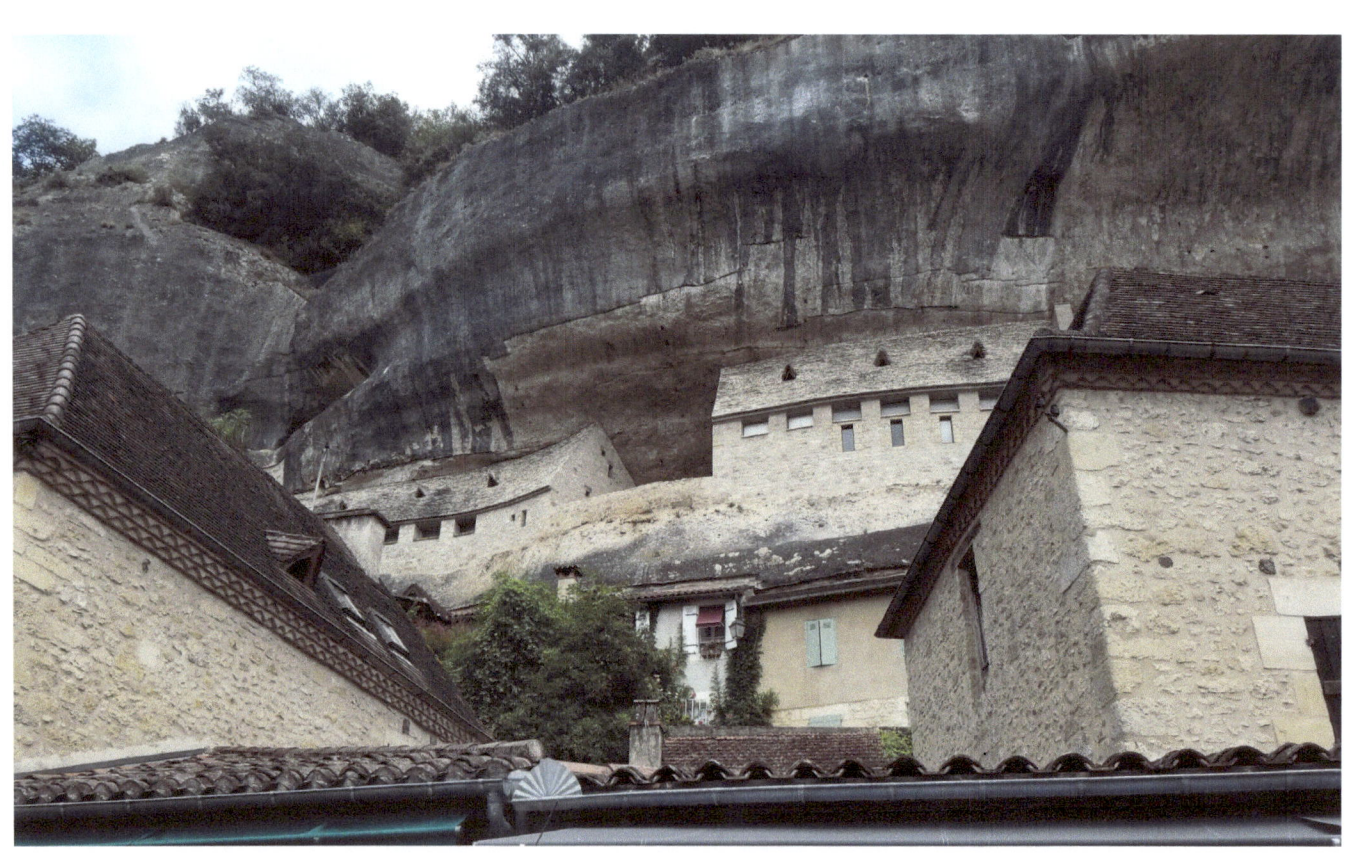

Driving through Sarlat-la-Caneda, in the Dordogne region, we were blown away by these prehistoric caves.

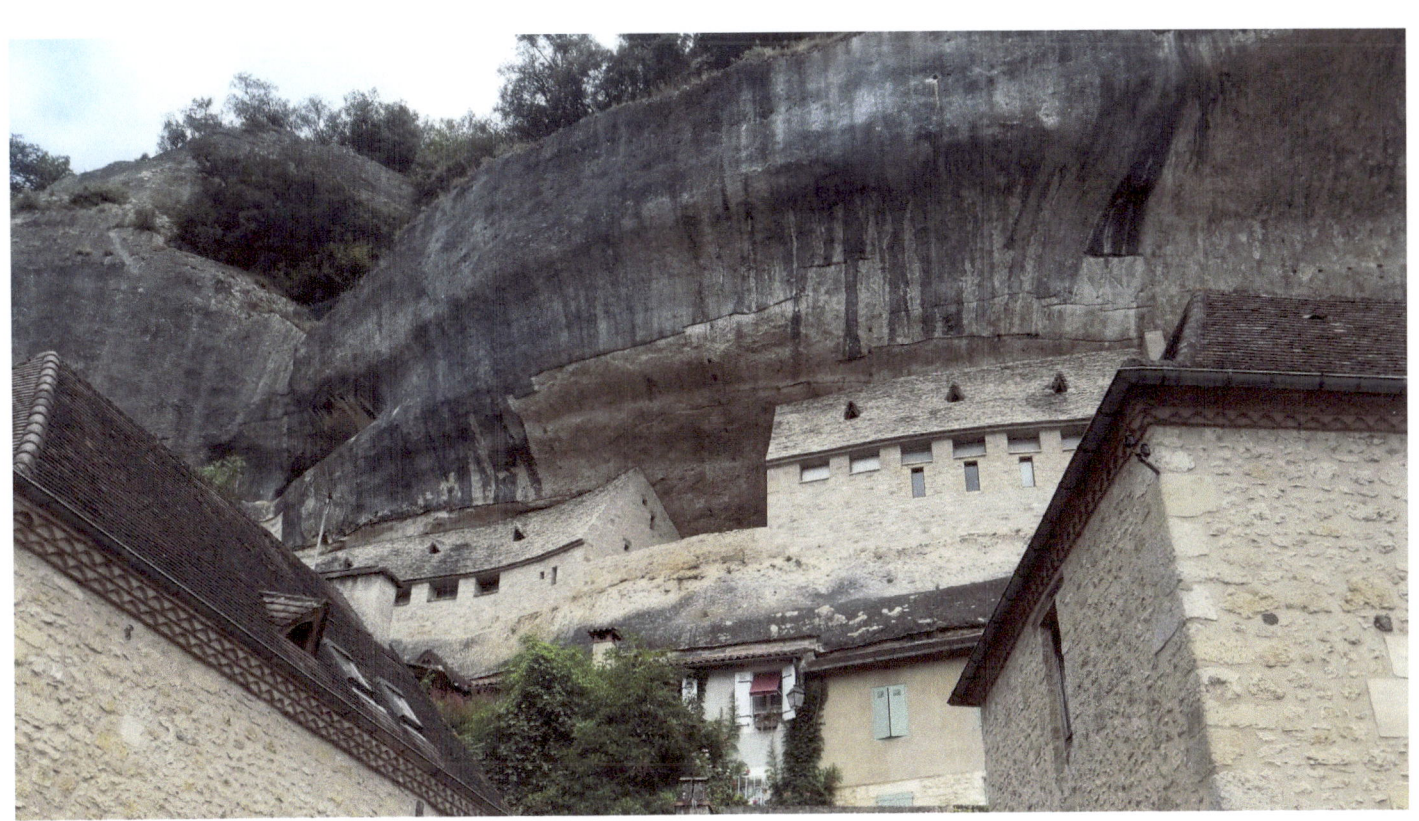

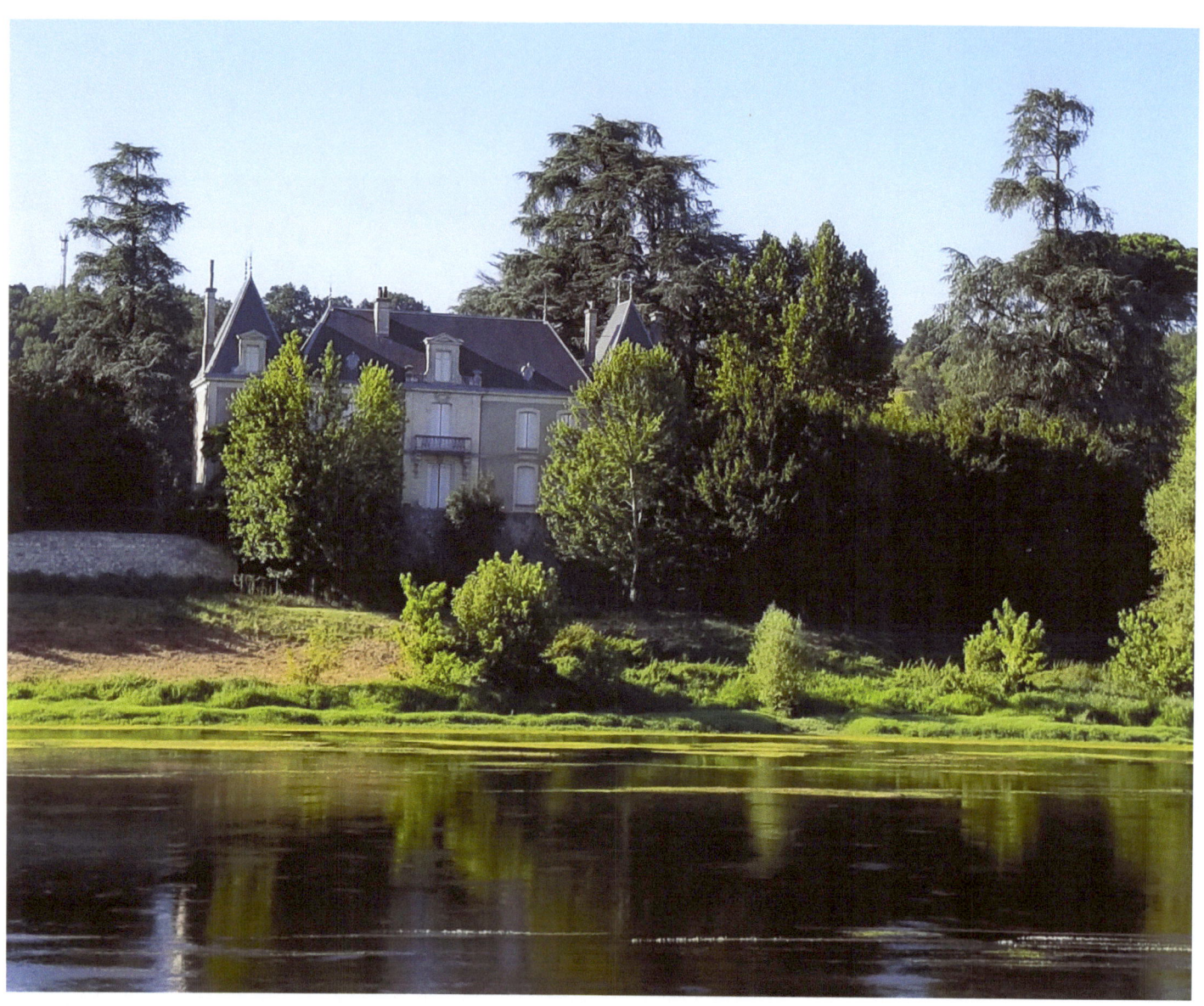

St Foy

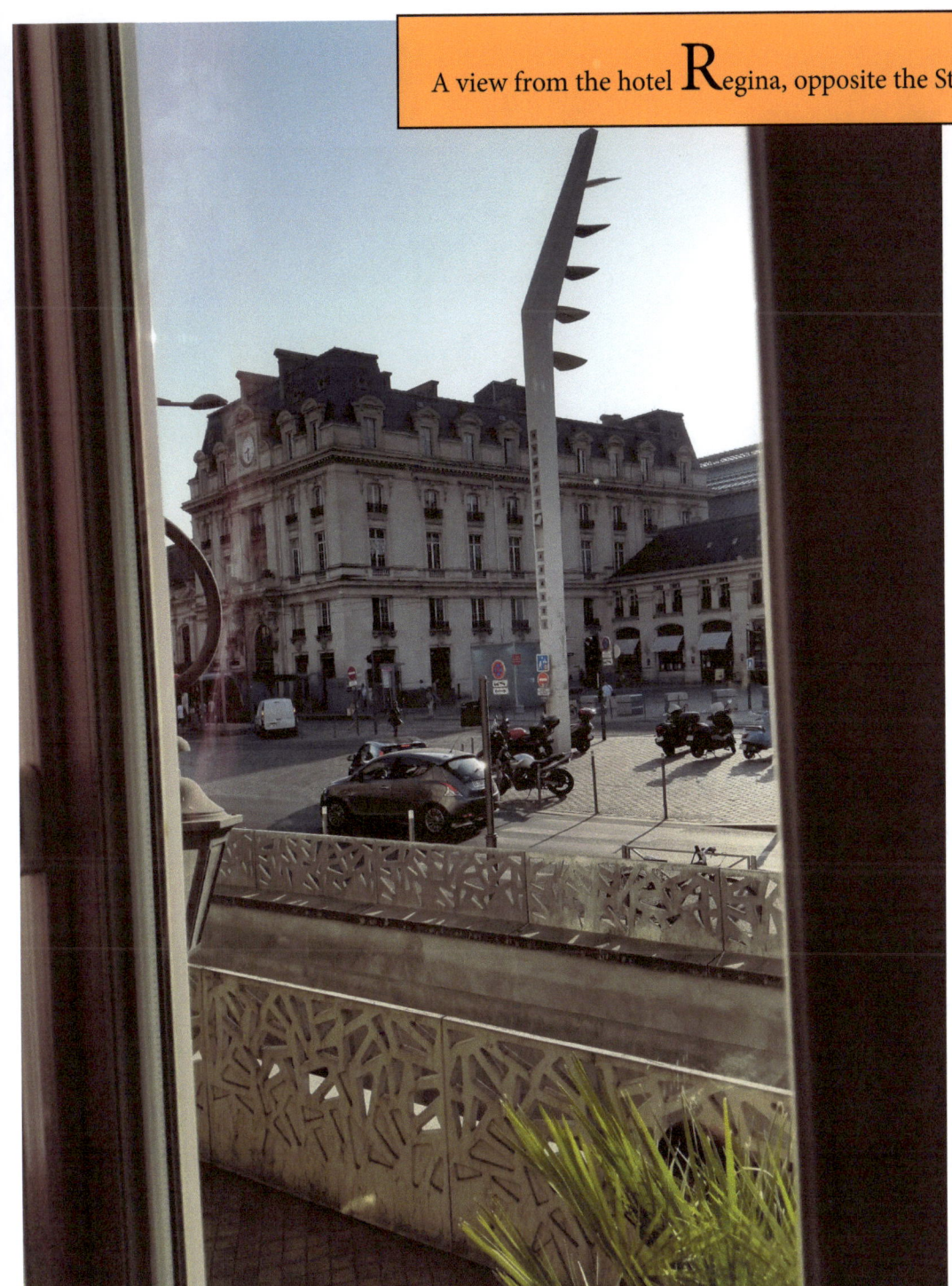

A view from the hotel Regina, opposite the St Jean Station in Bordeaux

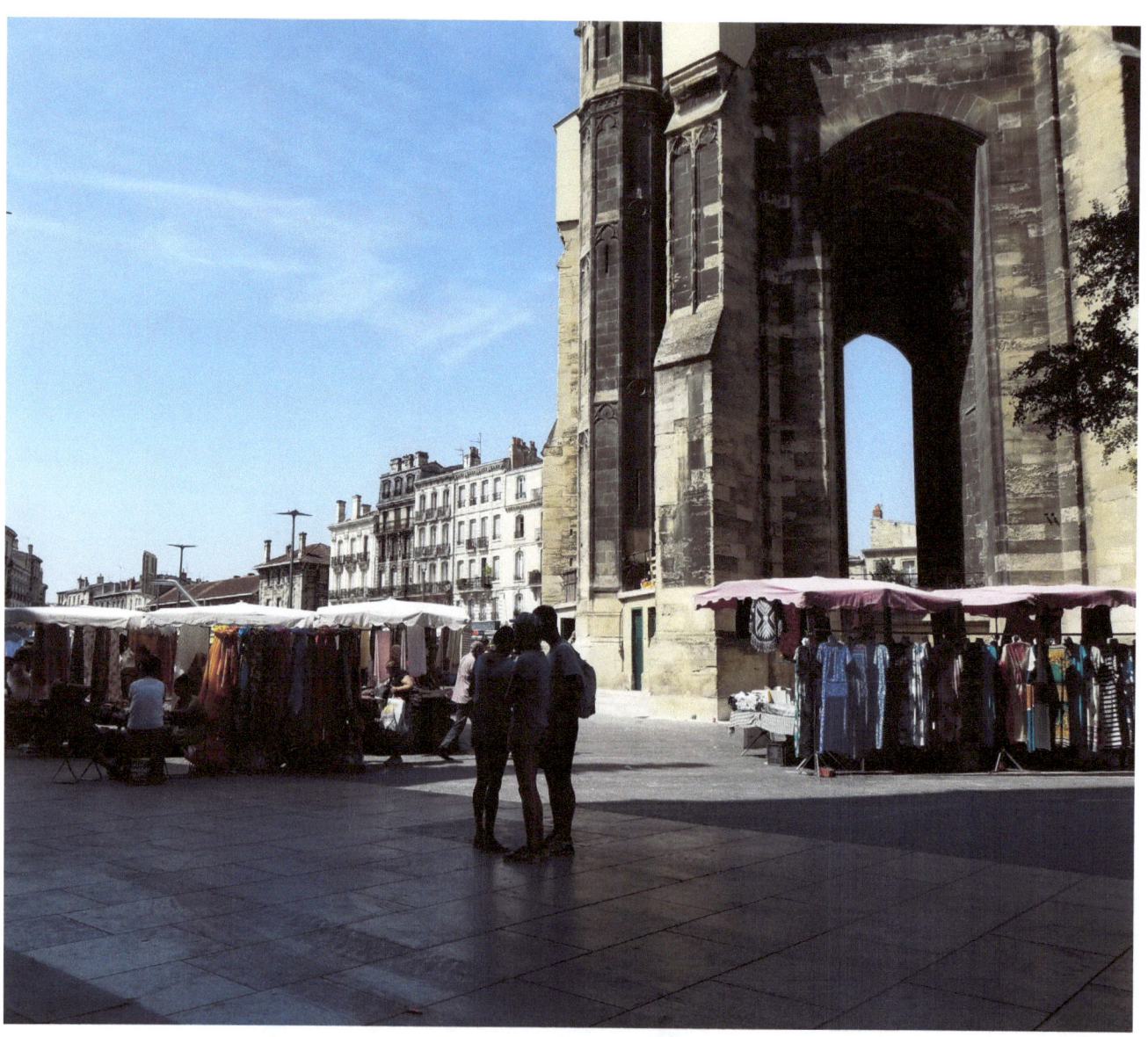

Bordeaux... Fighting the demons

Sometimes, if I narrow my focus within to only the sound of my heartbeat, I believe that I am invisible to the crowds around me. In fact, I believe that when they stare, they stare right through me, to whatever lies behind.

I am sitting on the small stone seat at the entrance of the Bordeaux Cathedral. Around the front of the church, there is a small market where vendors sell clothes and cloth, trinkets and organic soaps. Against the stoned walls and cobbled streets, brightly coloured cloths and dresses bellow in the breeze. It is 40 degrees celsius today and my second bottle of water has been consumed. My clothes are sticking on me, and I am from the Caribbean. I know heat, but not like this.

On the walk here from the Regina hotel, obliquely opposite the Bordeaux Train Station, the scents of the inner city stifled me. I guess it's the same anywhere you go. Concoctions of urine, food and sweat, especially in this heat.

Before I entered the Cathedral, I was met by Michel, who was busy asking for money. He was probably in his late sixties, and I started to chat with him a bit. His wife was dead, and he now calls the church his home. I guess, like cities, people are people, looking for connections, looking to belong to somewhere, to someone. So many of us spend our existence looking for that. What if we never find that, what then? The gargoyles high on the church stared at me something awful, and I averted my gaze.

Again I digress, so after the cathedral, we made our way down another street, but the heat caused us to stop. We spotted a small restaurant called "Brasserie Le Passage St Michel" with a few people sitting outside in the heat, sipping drinks. We went in and finally decided on lunch. It was actually one of the best meals we've had in France – ¼ poulet grille, haricots vert et carottes and for dessert, crème chocalat. The atmosphere was light and comfortable, and the waiter was so charming, we sat there for quite a while, and unwound.

What is it that make people connect and bond, while others remain strangers? I used to think it was some kind of commonality, be it attractiveness, similar likes, same culture, neighbourhood, friends. I sat back watching couples pass by, and I wonderd about my own choice of being relatively single. The thing about travelling is that it gives you time and space to ponder on everything that was buried, until you are left with the stench of unearthed emotions.

This is France, the country of love, and I am forced to battle my own demons. While many walk in pairs, I walk with my shadow, not really fitting in anywhere or with anyone, except at the newly found barber shop that was able to give me a decent mark. Now I can resemble a neater version of myself, as I prepare for Rome in the morning.

Italy

Rome - Old world architecture, Gods, the heat wave, millions of tourist and gelato

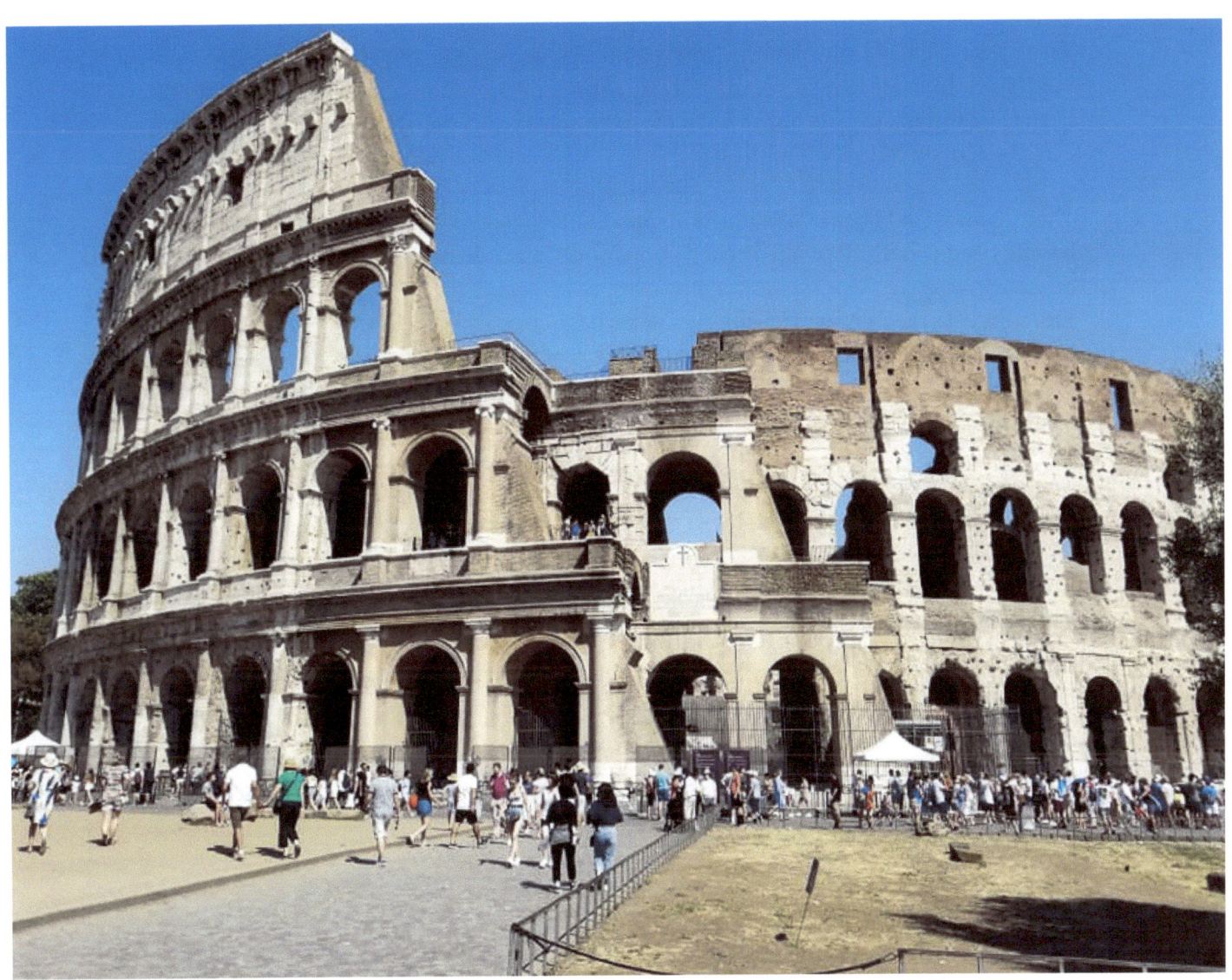

Observations

In France I felt a familiarity that relaxed me. Perhaps it was the smiles as people said- bonjour or bonsoir in a sing-song phrase, ending on a high note, reminiscent of home. Perhaps it was the connections I felt with some strangers, regardless of the sign language I used as currency to communicate.

Then again it could have been the familiar sounds of words, the spine to our own patois, having been colonized by the French at one time in our history.

From Paris to the Pyrenees feasting on wine, baguettes and the delicious French cuisine, eyes met across streets and train seats, while scenes zipped past like the memory this will one day be. Maybe there were negative whispers that I wasn't listening for, or didn't understand. Maybe life is filled with too many maybes... maybe I digress too often.

But Rome was different. A beautiful kind of different. Introspective and foreign as my thoughts bounced off stone, history and crazy driving.

Rome was majestic and statuesque like the Colosseum and the Pantheon -The meeting place for all Gods, before the majority of the world became monotheistic.

But even in that setting I felt that there was some harmony between the two doctrines of belief, even if it was only in architecture.

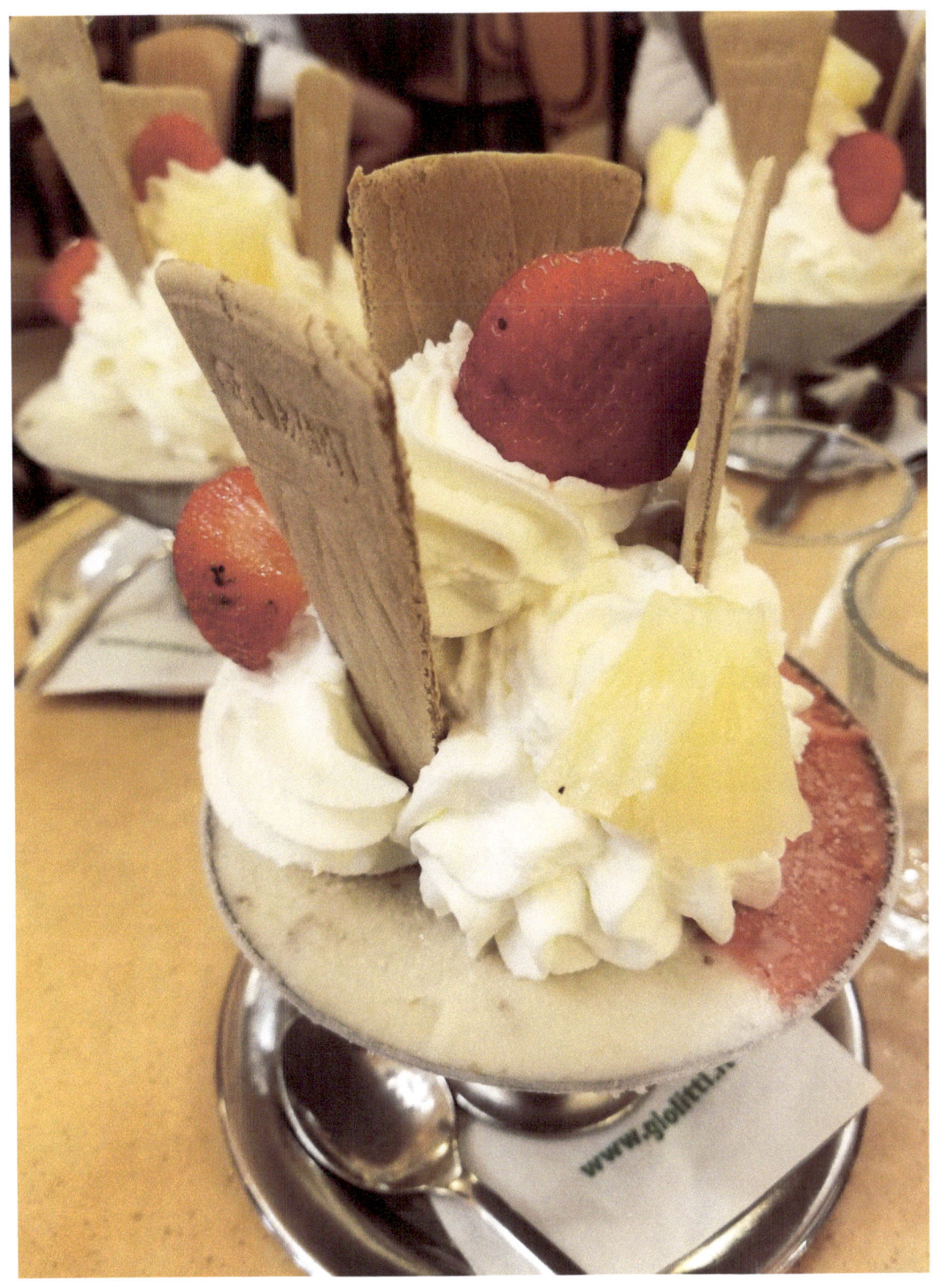

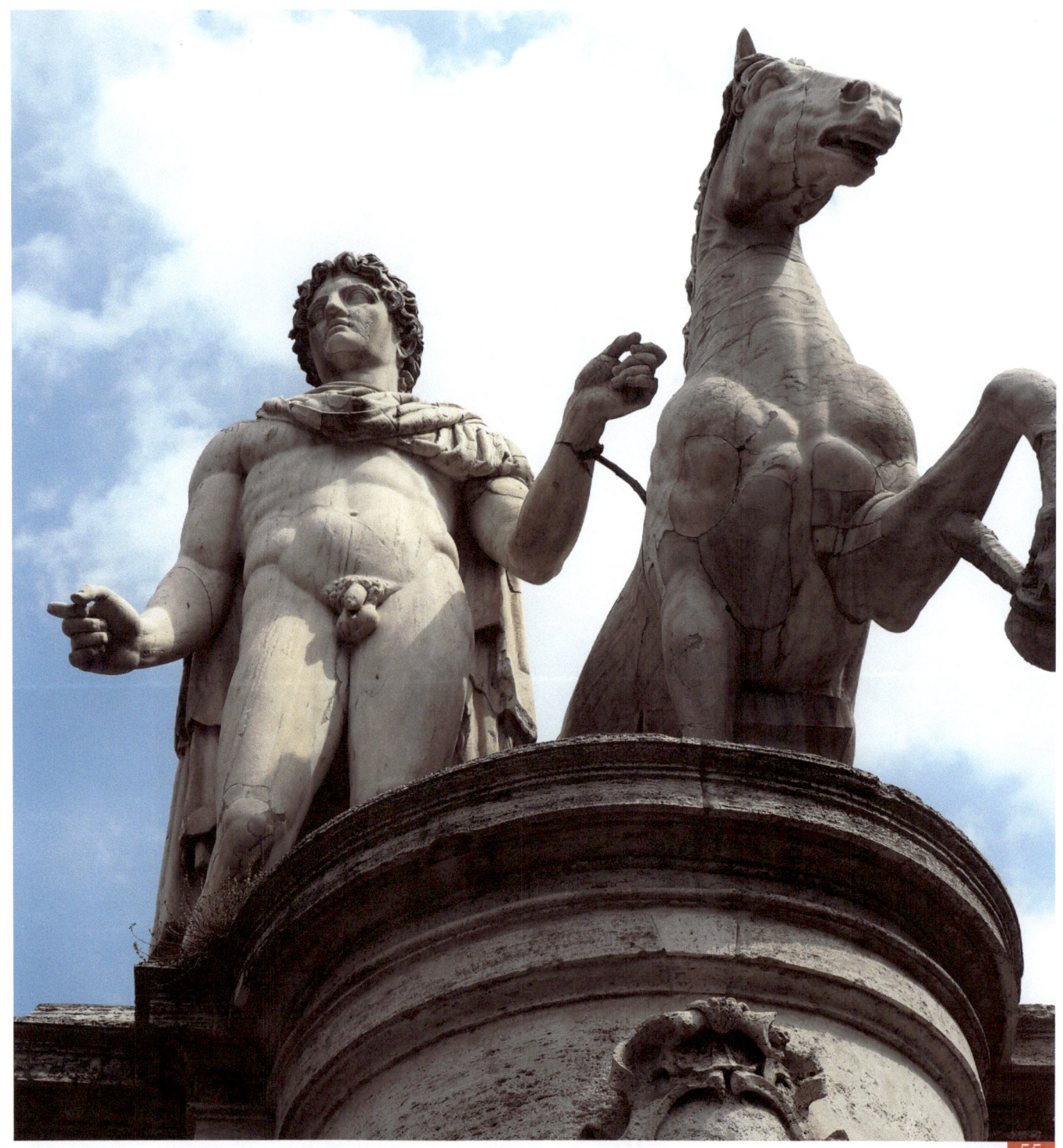

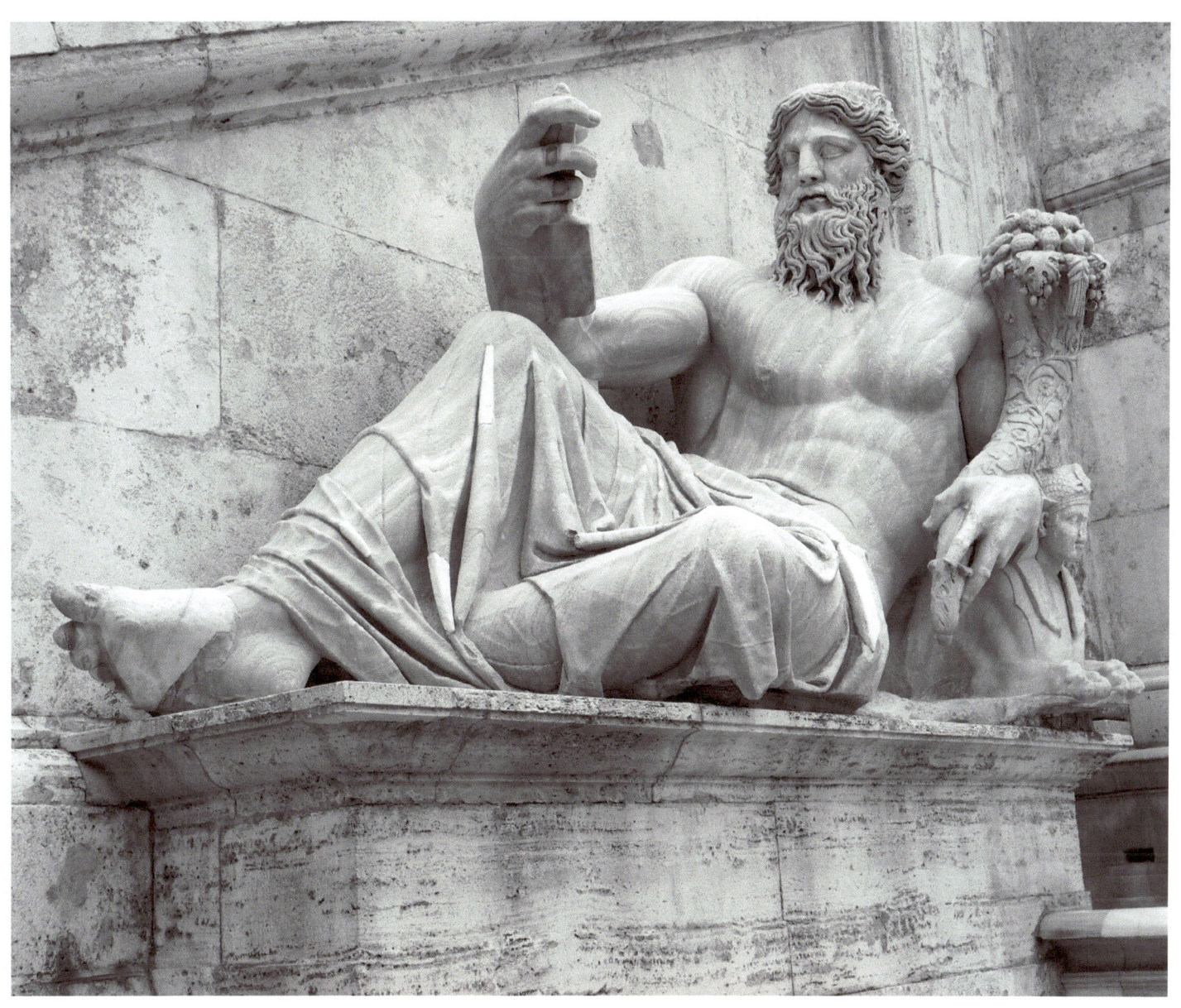

One of Michelangelo's ancient statues of a River God

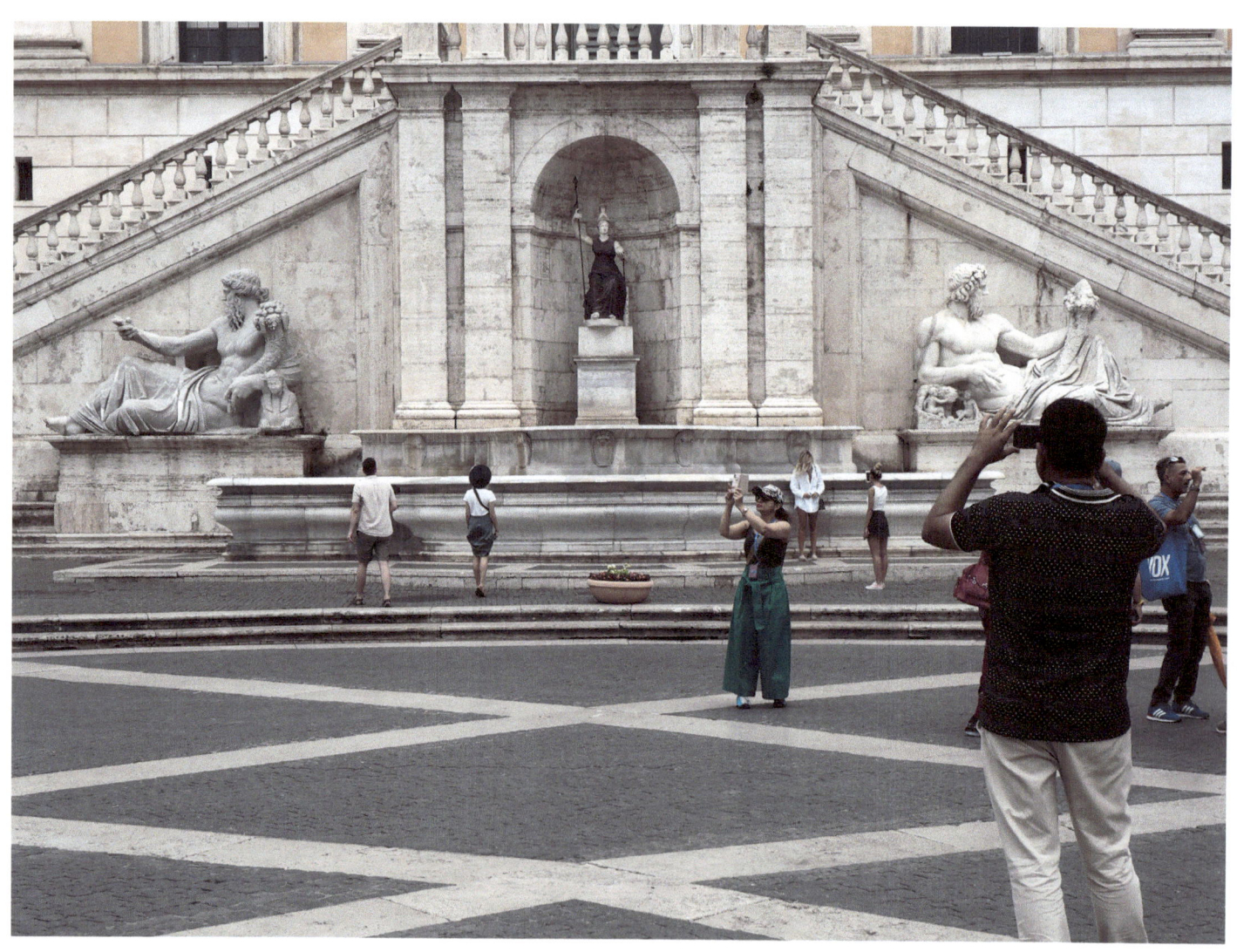

Statue of the Goddess Minerva between the two River Gods

Roman Forum

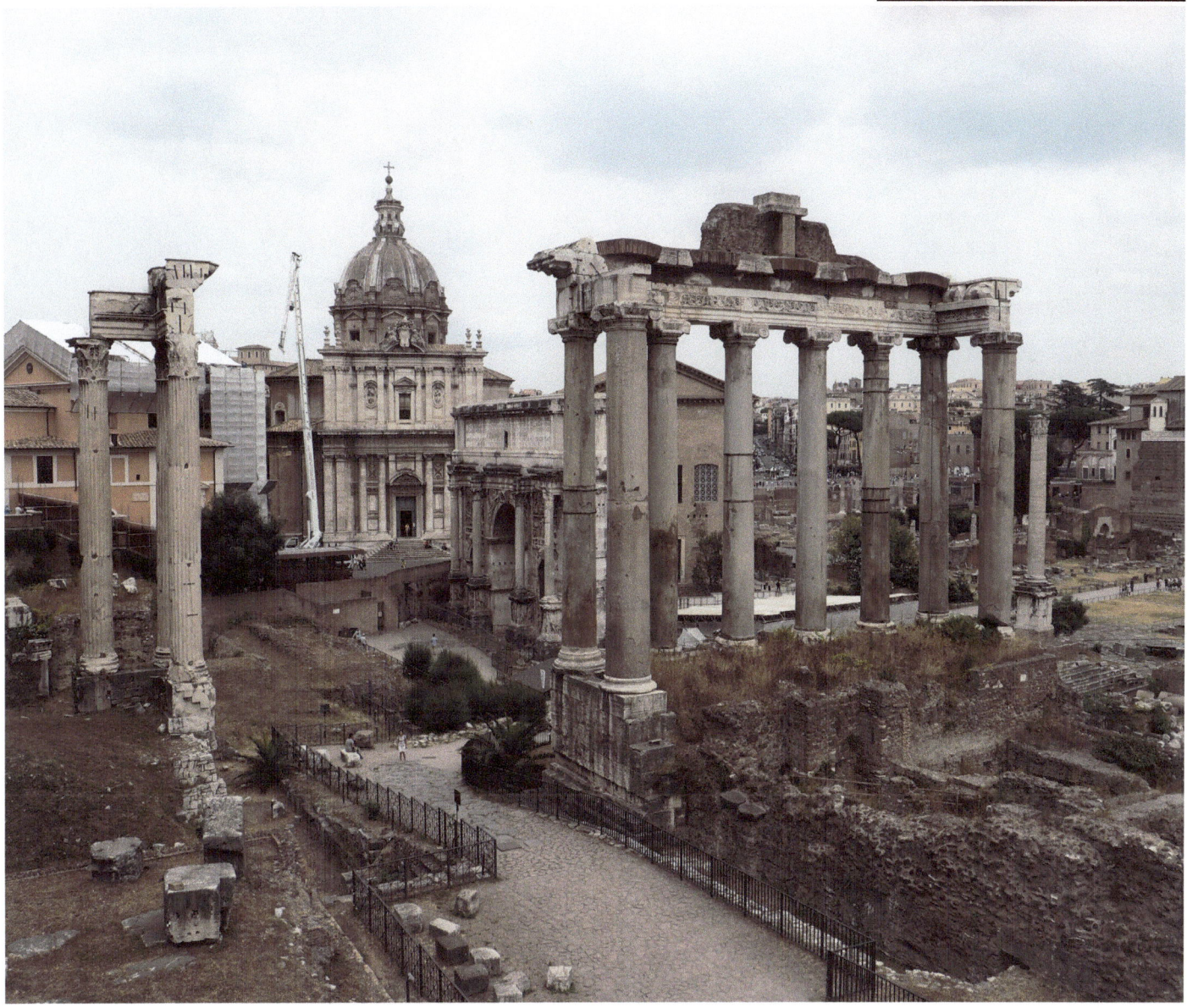

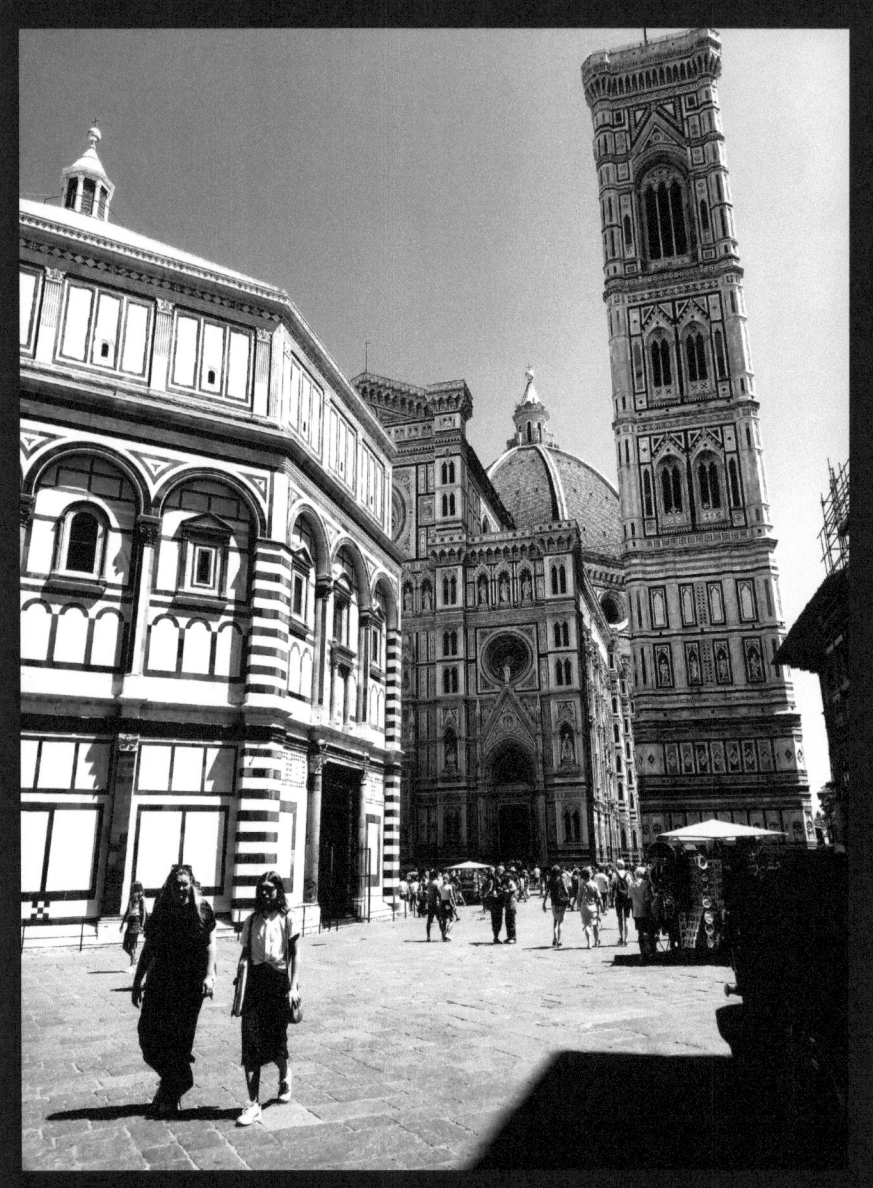

Florence

After catching a train in Rome to Florence I felt lost in a language and city. After extensive sign language and bits of various catch words, we got some direction.

Eventually after waiting for 15 minutes we boarded one of the buses many of the tourist hopped on to explore the inner city.

There were so many languages circling us, I grew silent and tired, but still in awe of the architecture and leather work.

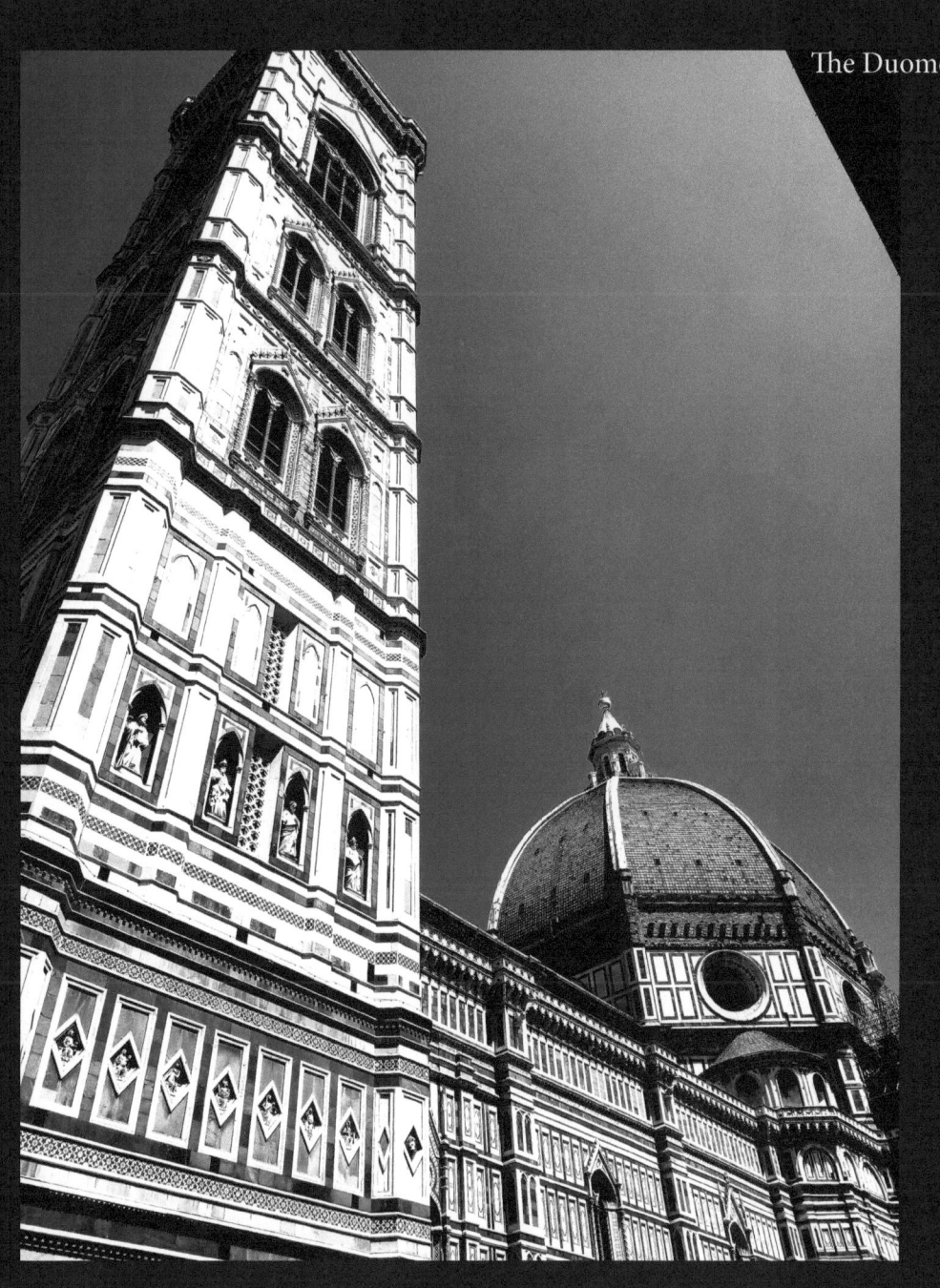
The Duomo in Florence

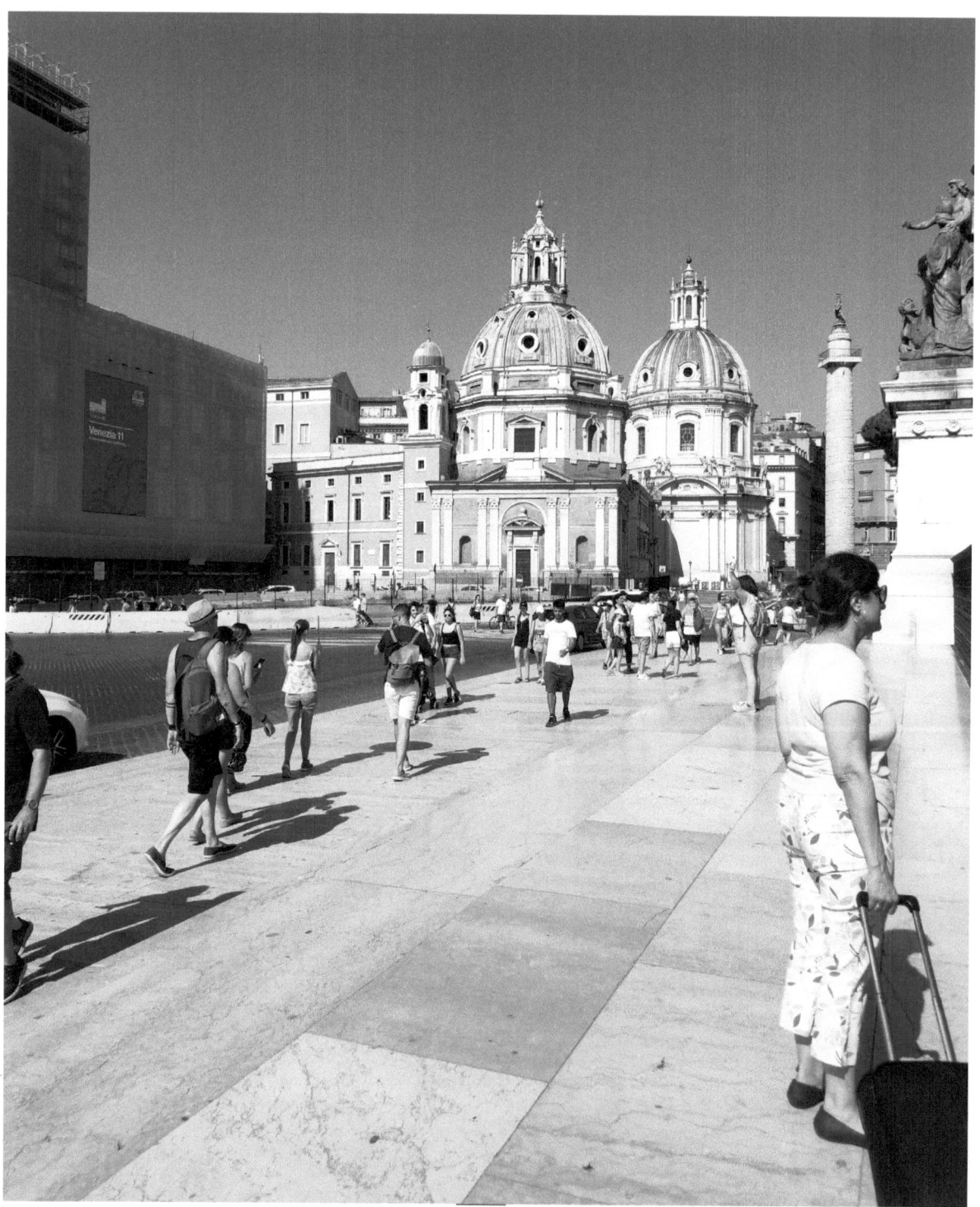

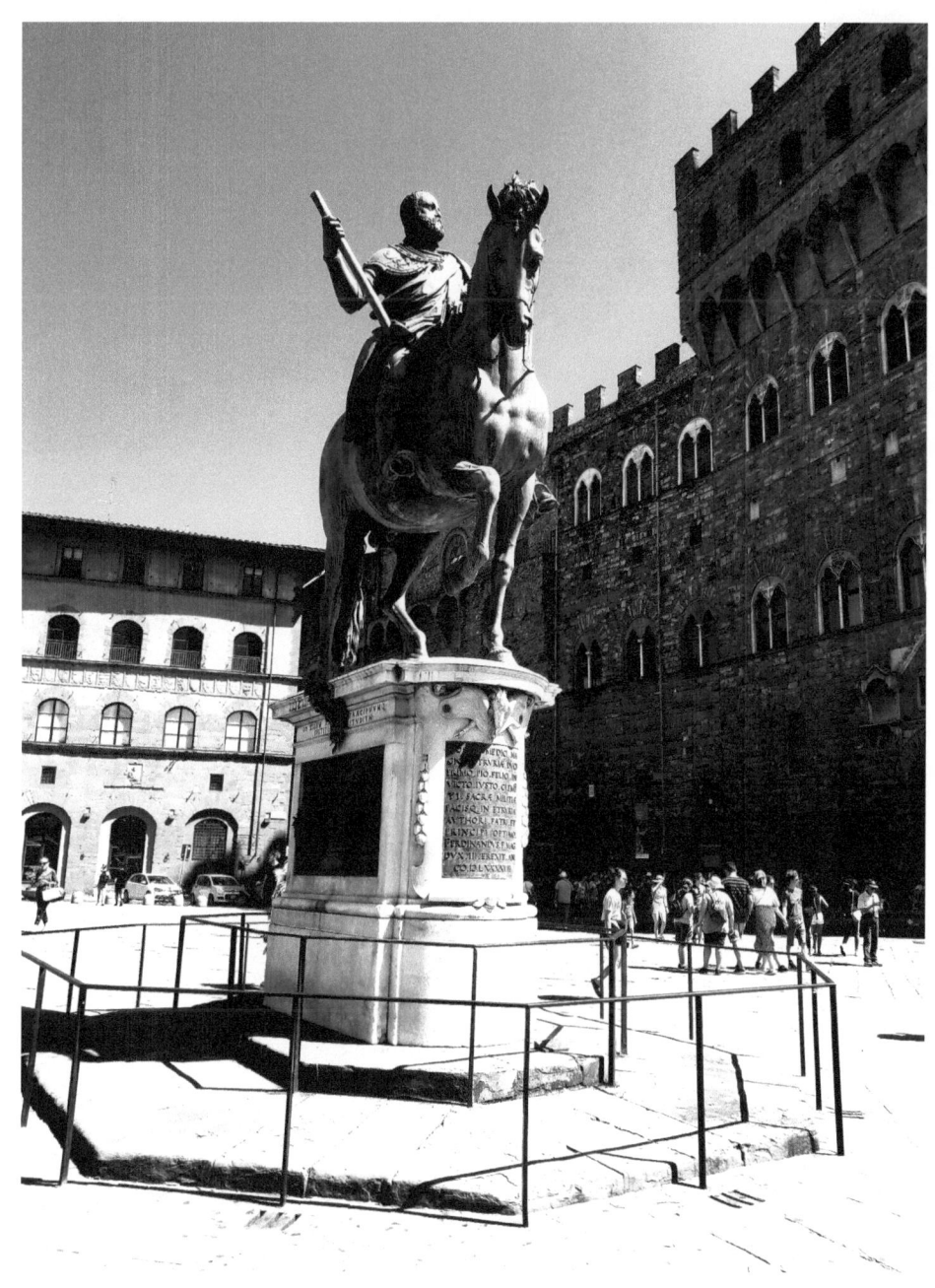

Monument of Cosimo 1 in Piazza della Signoria, Firenze Florence

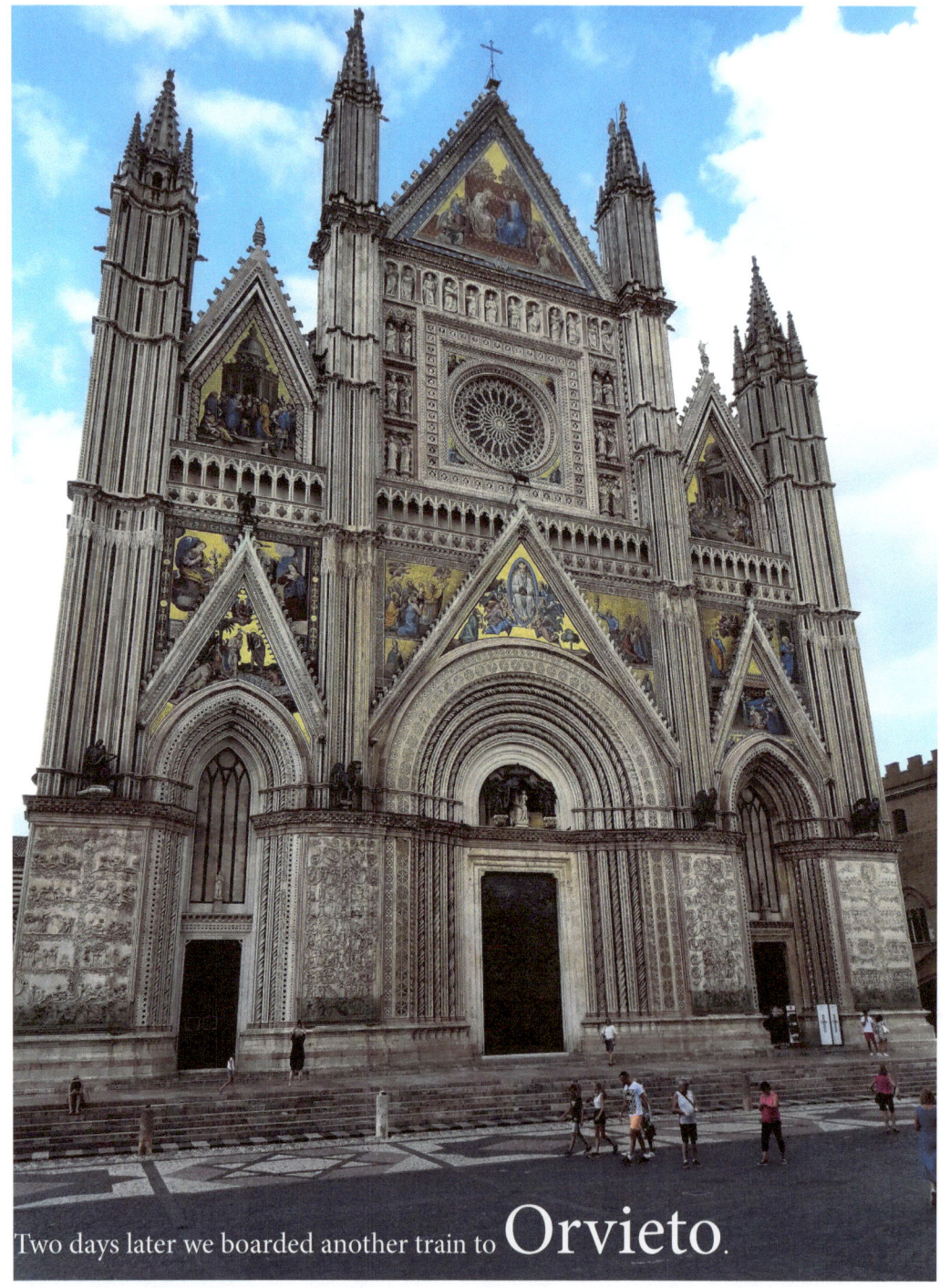

Orvieto Cathedral, 14th century Roman Catholic Cathedral.

Two days later we boarded another train to Orvieto.

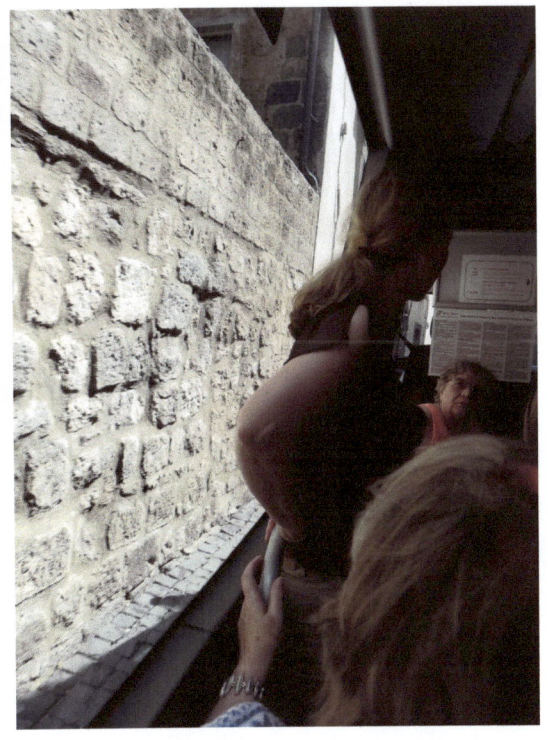

I believe that places, people and time are the only constants of change. They say no man is an island, but sometimes an island could be self sufficient, I suppose.

Yesterday we visited Orvieto, just outside of Rome. As the train pulled out of Roma Termini, a guy passed by selling water, beer, iced teas and soda from a small cooler.

As I sat drinking my beer and looking through the train's window, flashcards of buildings, and acres of land, vineyards and farm houses, passed by in moments that will soon be forgotten, once my life resumes its regular scheduled program. These flashcards reminded me of that old movie where the guy in the glass time machine watches years, and ages, and eons pass by in the blink of an eye.

After 90 minutes the train eventually stopped at our destination… Orvieto. It's the sparseness of people that reminded me of my own walls and space that I erect and demolish, as life permits.

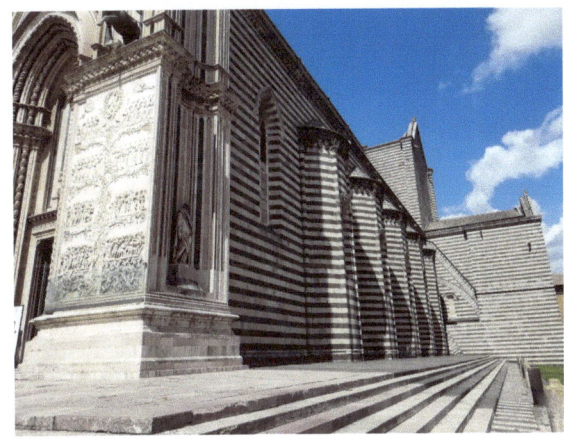

Once outside the train station, we cross the street to an almost empty row of tourist shops. Eventually, we got on board a tram cab that took us and several visitors uphill to what seemed like a small castle structure, surrounded by an empty lot with trees, a bus stop and a car park. We all waited on the free bus to take us around.

Twenty minutes later the bus arrived and we boarded. Someone should give that driver a medal! Through the narrowest streets I have ever seen, he maneuvered the vehicle between spaces where, not even a mosquito on a diet could have fitted alongside it! Some people gasped as we turned corners, as we became sandwiched between rocks and buildings, while I was sandwiched between thoughts, and even more thoughts.

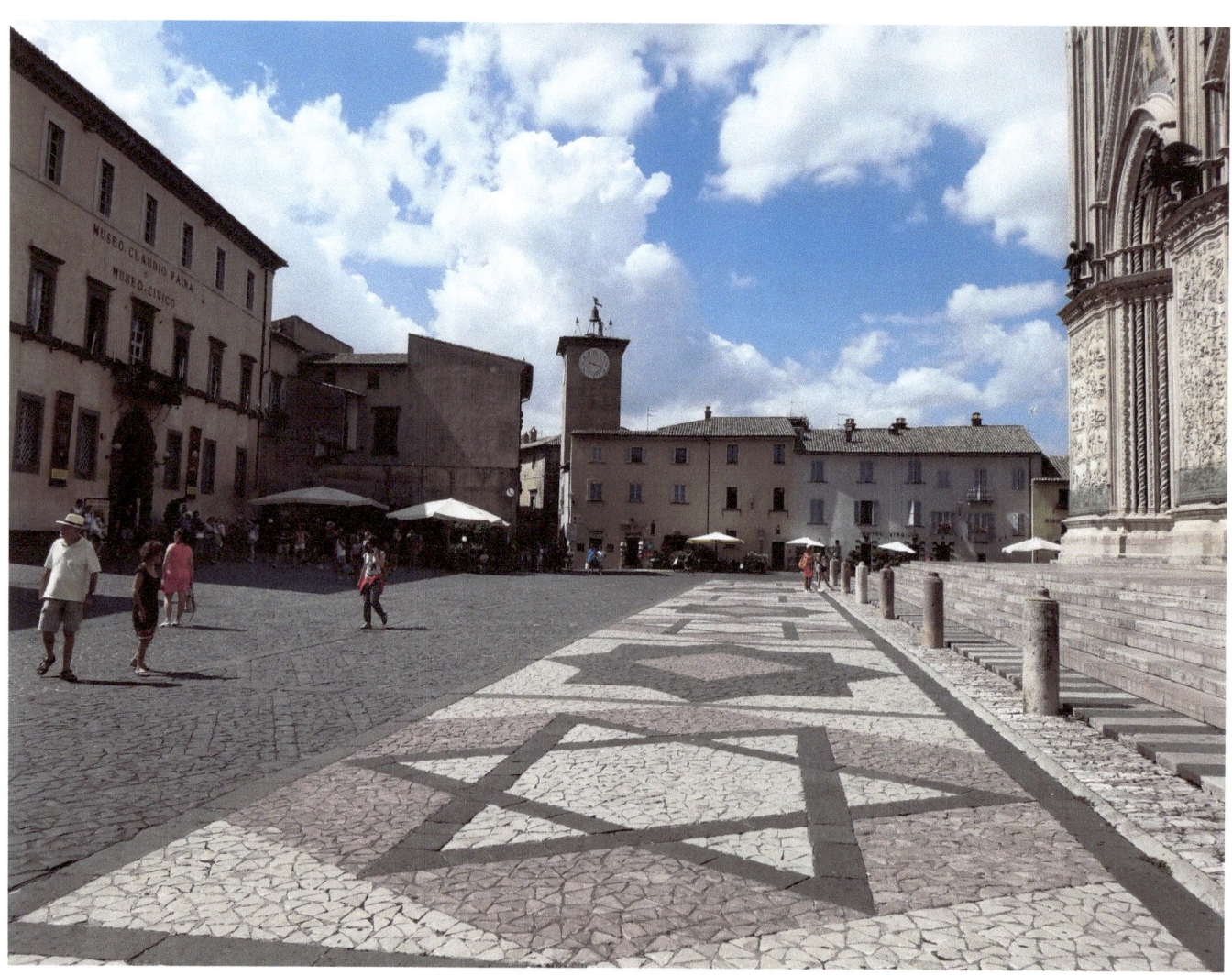

Orievto Cathedral Square

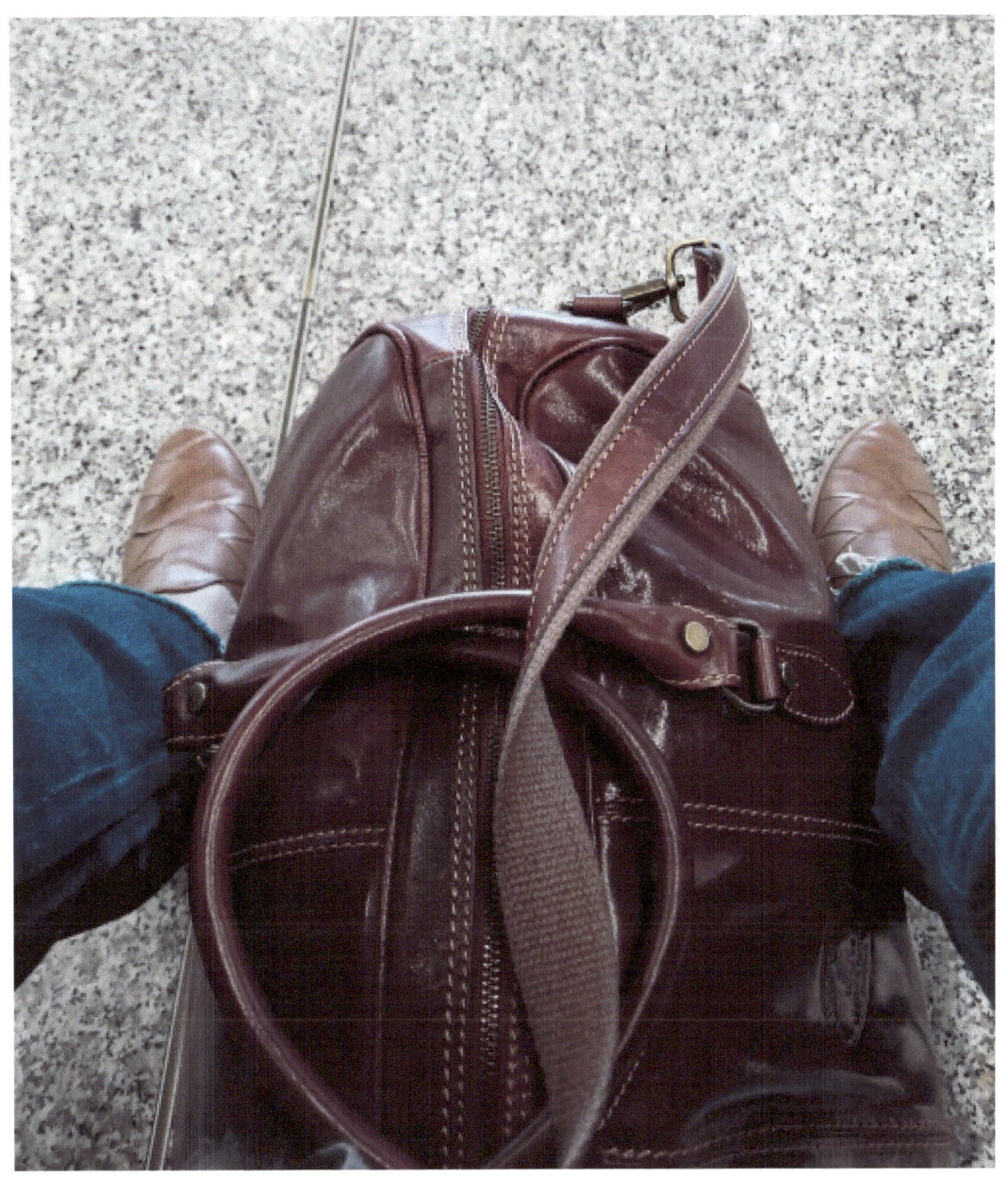

We said goodbye to Italy, and headed back to France for a week, before returning home. Every journey comes to an end.

Saying goodbye

Some journeys definitely stretch you in many directions, releasing inner demons while calming angels. This trip taught me things about myself and provided many still moments of reflection and awe, of wonder and yearnings and reaching out. Even if it was to feel the wind embracing me through my clothes.

This journey allowed me to say goodbye to a love that found me, while I lost it, then found it again, only to lose it in the end.

It was a journey of fitting in and standing out while standing apart from everything familiar.

It was a journey of beauty and inspiration of old world philosphies and new world thinking. Of sacred grounds and friendships, of mountains and cathedrals, smiles and tears, quiet cafes and elaborate buildings; of planes, automobiles, trains, buses, boats and worn sandals; of being close to home yet far away.
This journey brought me closer to me.

Thank you for accompanying me on my journey.

Paula Obe

www.ingramcontent.com/pod-product-compliance
Lightning Source LLC
Chambersburg PA
CBHW051202220526
45473CB00003B/876